Birdwatching in Ireland
with
Eric Dempsey

Birdwatching in Ireland
with
Eric Dempsey

Gill & Macmillan

Gill & Macmillan
Hume Avenue, Park West, Dublin 12
with associated companies throughout the world
www.gillmacmillan.ie

© Text, Eric Dempsey 2008, 2011
© Photographs, the individual photographers 2008, 2011
First published in hard cover 2008
First published in this format 2011

978 07171 5107 3

Index compiled by Cover To Cover
Design and print origination by Michael O'Clery
Printed in Malaysia

This book is typeset in Times New Roman, 11.25pt/14.8.

The paper used in this book comes from the wood pulp of managed forests.
For every tree felled, at least one tree is planted, thereby renewing natural resources.

A CIP catalogue record for this book is available from the British Library.

5 4 3 2 1

Title page: Robin (*Tom Cuffe*)

For Tom Dempsey, my father and my friend

Contents

Acknowledgments

Black Redstart *(Victor Caschera)*

So many people have given me encouragement and support that it is impossible to include all their names here. However, special mention must be given to Esther Murphy, Fergus Fitzgerald and Michael O'Clery — my birding partners, colleagues and friends for many years. Not only have we shared many wonderful experiences but their honest feedback and suggestions have also improved the contents of this book.

I would also like to thank Juanita Brown, Bryan Deegan, Geraldine Fisk, Anthony McGeehan and Roberta Reeners for their suggestions on early drafts, as well as Martin Garner, Kieran Grace, Niall Hatch, Aidan Kelly, Paul Milne, Killian Mullarney, Julie Roe and Steve Wing for their assistance.

To the members of the Tolka Branch of BirdWatch Ireland and the students in the People's College in Dublin, thanks for allowing me to develop so many topics on birds in such a relaxed and friendly atmosphere. Thanks also to Derek Mooney, Eanna ní Lamhna, Richard Collins, Terry Flanagan and Jim Wilson for many memorable bird broadcasts.

The text has been brought to life by the many wonderful images captured by Denise Bowden, Victor Caschera, Mícheál Casey, Derek Charles, Sean Cronin, Thomas Cuffe, Joe Curtis, Annette Cutts, Adrian Dancy, Michael Davis, Eddie Dunne, John Finn, Michael Finn, Terry Flanagan, John Fox, John Gallagher, Martin Garner, Paul Kelly, Matt Latham, Breffni Martin, Anthony McGeehan, Richard T. Mills, Killian Mullarney, Esther Murphy, Michael O'Clery, Michael O'Keeffe, Gearóid O'Sullivan, Valerie O'Sullivan, Lorcan O'Toole, Bill Quinn, Tom Shevlin, Clive Timmons and Mark Wilson. To say that I truly appreciate their creativity is an understatement. I would also like to thank the family of the late Warren Hewitt for kindly allowing me to use some of his superb images.

The 'Heritage in Schools Scheme' is something I am very pleased to be associated with and I would like to thank the staff of the Heritage Council and the INTO for their great work.

I would also like to take this opportunity to acknowledge the early influences of two teachers I had in national school. Thanks to Mrs McCarthy for taking her classes on nature walks long before nature studies was part of the school curriculum. Many generations of pupils have her to thank for their interest in the world around them. Thanks also to Brian Clarke for allowing me to discover that writing was fun.

Finally, I would like to thank my mother Ann and my family for their support and encouragement over the years.

Eric Dempsey

Preface

Peregrine *(Adrian Dancy)*

I have been birdwatching seriously for over 30 years. It seems like a very long time when I write it down, but believe me, those years have flown. Looking back, I now realise I didn't have a clue about what I was doing in the early days. It was only when I started meeting other birdwatchers that I slowly emerged from the darkness. It was a steep learning curve, but I began to understand the importance of having the right equipment and books, and to grasp the concept of migration. I also realised that the identification of birds requires constant study, whether you are an expert or a beginner. I am still learning — and we'll never know it all.

As I sat down to write this book, I found myself wondering what information would have been most useful to me when I was starting off. Indeed, what information had served me well for many years? The answers to these questions are found in the chapters of this book.

I have approached the subject in two distinct sections. The first part deals with all aspects of birds and birdwatching, while the second looks at bird identification in greater detail.

I hope this book steers you in the right direction from the very start and that the world of birds will continue to fascinate you for many, many years to come.

Introduction — Getting Started

(Clive Timmons)

Birdwatching is one of the most unpredictable but truly wonderful pastimes in the world. You can never be sure what you're going to see on any given day. Birds are always on the move and, according to the time of year or the weather conditions, the types of birds you see and their populations are ever-changing. There are few pastimes like it. Of course, taking that first step to observe the birds around you is just the

Species such as this Coal Tit readily come to gardens, and can be seen from your window. A pair of binoculars can greatly enhance the pleasure of watching birds up close
(Sean Cronin)

first in a journey that will bring wonderful experiences and hours of entertainment and pleasure. Birds are one of the most accessible forms of wildlife we have. Feeders in the garden in winter will attract finches from Scandinavia, while in summer Swallows that have wintered almost 10,000 km away in South Africa feed on insects over our fields and wetlands. Whether you simply watch birds in your garden or when out walking, or decide to go out with the specific intention of birdwatching, having an awareness of birds gives you a great sense of the changing seasons. Birds are also great indicators of change: they are usually the first to react to any environmental changes — good or bad.

Once you start observing birds you may find that you want to get a closer look at them. There comes a time when you have to admit to yourself … you need to buy a pair of binoculars. This is a very important step in your birdwatching journey and should not be rushed into.

There is a whole range of binoculars on the market these days, ranging in price from €20 to €2,000. The 'rule' of the most expensive being the best doesn't always apply. There are many modestly priced, top-class makes of binoculars available. However, the rule usually works in reverse — the cheapest pairs of binoculars usually are the worst.

To begin with, it is necessary to understand what makes a good birdwatching pair of binoculars. There

1

are several main things to consider. First, the binoculars should be reasonably lightweight — remember, these could be hanging around your neck for ten hours at a time. So the binoculars should feel light and comfortable. Secondly, they need to be powerful enough to see the birds clearly but also bright and sharp enough to see colours and colour definitions accurately (are the legs on that bird grey or pale blue?). Lastly, most binocular lenses have several layers of chemical coatings to protect both the lenses and, more importantly, your eyes. Remember, if you're out birdwatching on a sunny day, you may well be exposing your eyes to severe glare and may even suffer 'eyeburn' (my word for sunburnt eyes). Cheaper binoculars not only give poor colour definition but many do not offer the same protection for your eyes as the more expensive, better designed models. If you're going to embark on this birdwatching journey, you need to look after your eyes.

Choosing a pair of binoculars is a very personal thing, but the following is a brief guide on what to look for.

Magnification: When choosing a pair of binoculars, try out different magnifications. All binoculars show a symbol of **7x** or **8x** or **10x** etc. This simply means that you're seeing things magnified 7 times (the x) or 8 times or 10 times. For birdwatching, 7 or 8 magnification is ideal; 10x binoculars are also very good, but many 10x binoculars tend to be heavier and, as a result, any small hand tremor is very obvious when looking through them. At all costs, avoid anything bigger than 10x: what you gain in magnification, you lose in light and quality of image.

Lens size: This refers to the size of the big lens at the end of the binoculars (i.e. the objective lens). The size of the objective lens is usually given after the magnification on binoculars. Therefore a pair of **7x42** binoculars has a **magnification of 7 times** and an **objective lens size of 42 mm**. The golden rule is that the bigger the lens size, the more light it allows in.

However, the amount of light also depends on the magnification of the binoculars you are using. There is a simple calculation you can use: **divide the lens size by the magnification**. Therefore, a pair of 7x42 binoculars is 42 divided by 7, which equals 6 (6 = the

Using binoculars can help you identify distant birds. Here, a Bar-tailed Godwit, flying with a flock of Sanderling *(Adrian Dancy)*

light intake of the binoculars). The higher that number, the more light you have, e.g. 8x42 = 42/8 = 5.25; 10x50 = 50/10 = 5 etc. In this case, 7x42 binoculars allow more light into the eye, so the image you see will be brighter.

There is one last consideration, and it depends on the amount of money you wish to spend. In most binoculars, brightness is reduced slightly when the light enters the lens and is bounced off several mirrors before reaching your eyes. The more times this happens, the less bright and sharp is the image. This is how most binoculars are designed and they are called Porro Prisms. There are other designs, however, called Roof Prisms (or 'straight through') binoculars. These are usually the most expensive makes because they are designed to allow the light to pass 'straight through' the lens and into your eyes, making the image brighter and sharper.

Ultimately, the type of binoculars you choose is entirely a personal choice. Before buying them, try them out. Make sure they feel comfortable. Check to see how close they focus. Does the focus wheel turn smoothly? If you wear spectacles, it's important to check whether the eyecups (where you look through) adjust to allow you to use the binoculars while wearing your spectacles. Can you see yourself having these around your neck for ten hours? Do they feel right for you?

Some people opt for the really small makes of binoculars, the type you can carry in your top pocket. Using binoculars that are tiny may help with avoiding neck strain, but you might as well tape two Smarties boxes together and cover the ends with cellophane for all that you will see with them — unless, of course, you purchase the most expensive makes. But even then, if you're willing to pay the high prices for the best models, it makes more sense to get the best size for birdwatching while you're at it.

Big binoculars that have zoom lenses can be as bad. How can you start getting to know birds when the image you're seeing is blurred and in near darkness? Once again, what you gain in magnification, you lose in image quality and brightness. The only advantage to these big binoculars is that you'll develop wonderful neck and arm muscles from carrying them around your neck and lifting them up to your eyes!

While I'm on the subject, let me mention the straps you use to carry your binoculars. Many good binoculars come with wide, padded straps. These allow you to wear your binoculars around your neck

Porro prism binoculars *(Esther Murphy)*

Roof prism binoculars *(Esther Murphy)*

comfortably for hours. Anyone who wears heavy binoculars supported by narrow, plastic straps will quickly realise just how uncomfortable they can be (severe rope burn doesn't come close). Good padded straps on your binoculars allow for a more comfortable time when out birdwatching. In the USA, birdwatchers get over the problem of neck strain by using a harness to support their binoculars. The harness is attached to the binoculars, goes over the shoulders and is clipped into place at the back. For me, these 'bra-like' straps make perfect sense in that they do prevent neck strain. However in my opinion, they really only suit warm climates. I can't imagine myself wearing such a harness over layers of fleece jackets and raingear in an Irish winter. Having said that, there are many people who swear by them. Like the binoculars themselves, the kind of straps you choose to wear is entirely a personal thing. If it feels right for you … then it's right.

My final piece of advice is perhaps stating the obvious: it's always best to go into a reputable shop and spend time talking about your choice and requirements. Make sure you're allowed to try out the binoculars. Do a little research on the makes and designs. Each pair of binoculars has an adjustment that allows it to adapt to each user's eyesight. Ask the shop assistants to show you how to adjust your binoculars to suit your eyes (if he/she doesn't know how to do that, then he/she is either very bad at his/her job or it's not a good shop). If you meet other birdwatchers, ask for their opinions on the different models; better still, ask for a look through their binoculars. You'll find that most people you meet are very willing to share their experiences and give advice.

In summary, a half-decent pair of binoculars with a comfortable strap will get you off on the right footing … at least you will be able to see what you're looking at, and that's a start.

Now that you have your binoculars, you are armed with the right equipment to go out birdwatching. As you become more experienced, you'll find that your binoculars become part of you, and after a while you won't even notice you have them around your neck. For many, though, binoculars are just the start of the equipment. When you want to figure out what those grey dots feeding on the mudflats are, you will realise that it's time for a serious commitment … and will consider purchasing a telescope.

Using a telescope or binoculars can open up a whole new world of birdwatching *(Adrian Dancy)*

An angled telescope, mounted on a sturdy tripod *(Esther Murphy)*

Like binoculars, telescopes come in all price ranges and in many sizes. However, the same general rules apply to telescopes as to binoculars. So, the bigger the objective lens, the brighter the image will be. The higher the magnification, the duller the image will be. Many telescopes have interchangeable eyepieces so you can have a choice of a zoom or a fixed lens. A good zoom would be perhaps 20x–60x, allowing you to increase the magnification from 20x to 60x. The higher end of the zoom can be quite dull, but can often allow you to see some feature on a bird that you would otherwise never see. A 'fixed' lens is one that has a fixed magnification (i.e. it does not zoom from one magnification to another); many people opt for a '32x wide-angle'. This gives you a magnification of 32x, but also widens the field of view. Put simply, a wide-angle eyepiece gives you a wider image than a zoom eyepiece does. There is no right or wrong — it's entirely a matter of personal choice. In fact, many people purchase both a zoom and a fixed eyepiece and change them according to their needs.

There are also different styles of telescope: some have angled bodies, so that you look down into the eyepiece; others have a straight body so you look straight through the eyepiece. Both are equally good and the choice is entirely yours. Personally, I've always favoured an angled telescope because I find it more relaxing to simply look down into my eyepiece. Most good telescopes are quite expensive, so before you buy one, be sure to do a little research, speak with other birdwatchers and go to a reputable shop. At this point, it's worth noting that most astronomical telescopes (with the exception of a very few expensive and compact makes) are not very good for birdwatching — they are often too large and too cumbersome to use in the field.

One other thing to remember is that when you buy a telescope, you'll need to buy a tripod as well. There is no point having a wonderful telescope if it is balanced on a flimsy tripod that shakes in the slightest wind. Your tripod will also need to be easy and comfortable to use. Tripods come in two parts: the legs and the head. The legs should be sturdy and, when fully opened, should be a comfortable height to allow you to look though your telescope without any difficulty. The legs are telescopic in design, usually having three sections that fold into one another. Make sure the clips that hold each section in place are easy to open and close. You don't want to be wasting too much time opening and closing the legs of your tripod every time you want to look at a bird. Some of these clips are also as deadly as a mousetrap, snapping shut very quickly and catching fingers in the process (show me a birdwatcher who has not at some time suffered the excruciating pain of having a finger caught in a tripod!). So check to ensure you're not buying a 'mousetrap tripod'. The second part of the tripod is the 'head', which is where the telescope sits. The movement of the head should be smooth and it should be easy to use. Many heads are designed for use with video cameras and are called 'floating heads'. These are excellent because they allow a very fluid and smooth movement. With a telescope, all you need is a movement that goes up and down, and left and right. So choose a simple type of head with no more than two knobs to control these movements. Some heads have so many knobs and handles that you'll spend hours just trying to figure out how to move your telescope from side to side. These might be great for photographers who want different angles etc. but are not helpful for birdwatching.

My final piece of advice when it comes to choosing a telescope and tripod is to consider the weight. Many people will buy the best equipment, but then discover that it is too heavy to carry. Naturally, some telescopes are bigger and heavier than others. The larger and heavier ones usually have a bigger objective lens, which means they are brighter than the smaller ones: this is the trade-off. Some expensive tripod legs are made of graphite, making them lighter than other makes. Many people are now choosing a heavier telescope but with a graphite tripod, which helps to reduce the weight. Be sure to check the weight of the equipment and choose the size of telescope and the make of tripod that suits you best.

Of course, now that you can see birds clearly with your binoculars or telescope, it is time to identify those birds, and to do that you will need a good book

Some of the best bird books to get: *The Complete Guide to Ireland's Birds*; *Finding Birds in Ireland*; *The Pocket Guide to the Common Birds of Ireland* and *The Collins Bird Guide*. The first three cover Ireland. The Collins Guide covers Europe, North Africa and the Middle East.

on birds. There are many, many field guides on the shelves of all good bookshops, but the problem is that they vary widely both in quality and information. If you're just beginning to discover the wonders of Irish birds, you'll quickly find that some books can be quite misleading because they include bird species that do not occur in Ireland. For example, Tawny Owls, Nuthatches and Green Woodpeckers aren't found in Ireland, yet many books refer to them as being common woodland species. Therefore, it's a good idea to buy a book that deals specifically with Ireland's birds. It is important to choose a book that will provide as much information on the identification of Ireland's birds, as well as their status in Ireland and the habitats in which they are found. I am, of course, rather biased, but for these reasons I would recommend either *The Complete Guide to Ireland's Birds* or *The Pocket Guide to the Common Birds of Ireland*, both by Eric Dempsey and Michael O'Clery and published by Gill & Macmillan. Another book, *Finding Birds in Ireland — The Complete Guide* by the same authors is also a must for any Irish birdwatcher because it gives details of all the best birdwatching sites in Ireland, when to visit them, how

A perfect example of what to wear *(Clive Timmons)*

A perfect example of what *not* to wear *(Clive Timmons)*

to get there and, most important of all, what you might expect to see when on your visit.

If you want a more concise European bird identification guide, then the best is the *Collins Bird Guide* by Mullarney, Svensson, Zetterström and Grant. This includes many birds that you'll never see in Ireland, and covers every species of bird found in Europe, North Africa and the Middle East.

Avoid the big coffee-table books that have titles like 'All the Birds of the World'. While they may be nice to browse, most of these books simply show the brightest birds in the world, but will be of very little help when you are trying to identify that small brown bird in your back garden.

When we speak of the equipment needed for birdwatching, we usually concentrate on the likes of binoculars, telescopes and books, but the type of clothing you use is equally important. Ireland can be a wet and cold place, so warm, waterproof clothing is a must. However, most waterproof clothing seems to come in the brightest and noisiest materials ever

invented. Birds, by their nature, are shy and retiring, and they also have great eyesight and good hearing. Bright orange and yellow jackets that are designed to be seen by mountain rescue teams 10 km away are not exactly the ideal colours to wear when out birdwatching. Likewise, these types of jacket also seem to make the loudest noise. Every movement you make generates enough sound and vibrations to register on the Richter scale. Let's face it … if you wear such clothing, every bird from here to Timbuktu will have seen and heard you coming from kilometres away. So the rule of thumb for birdwatching is subtle colours and not too noisy!

Regardless of whether you choose to be a very active outdoor birdwatcher or are just interested in the birds you see in your garden every day, there is one final piece of advice I would like to offer: take note of what you see. I have been an avid note-taker since the very first moment I started taking an interest in birds. It's great to look back over old notebooks. They are documented moments of discovery for you. Notes

Keep a notebook of your sightings. What date do you see your first Swifts each year? *(Adrian Dancy)*

don't need to be complicated or too detailed — they can be kept in a diary-style format or even on a computer spreadsheet. Some things I always include in my notes are the date, the location and the birds I've seen. If visiting a new habitat, I'll often include a brief note on that, too. Such notes can be very useful and allow direct comparisons to be made year after year. By simply taking note of the date you see your first Greenfinches return to your garden in winter, or when the Blue Tit family left the nest-box, and then comparing that date with the previous year(s), you can sometimes find an emerging pattern. Even simple notes can show if birds like Swallows and Swifts are arriving earlier or later each spring, or if they are staying later each autumn.

It is also worth documenting the birds you see in your garden or when out birdwatching. This builds into a very valuable record of what you have seen. I would suggest that you also take note of the features you see on birds. By taking note of the features you have seen, the physical act of writing it down reinforces those key features in your mind. It's also a good idea to take note of where you are and perhaps even the type of habitat you've visited. If in a

woodland, take note of whether it was deciduous or coniferous. This simple note will quickly demonstrate the different birdlife you can expect to find in different places.

As weather conditions can have a dramatic effect on bird movements, I also jot down some simple notes on the weather whenever I go out. I usually note such things as the wind direction and general notes on whether it was wet, sunny or cold. By noting the weather, you will see that certain birds turn up at certain times of the year following certain weather conditions. Your notes can act as a very valuable reference. At this stage, I can almost predict when I will see Siskins in my garden each winter by looking at the weather that brought them into my garden in previous years. When I see a similar weather forecast, I know that Siskins should arrive … and most times they do.

So, now that you have your binoculars, and perhaps even a telescope, as well as your field guide, a notebook and dull, quiet clothes, it's time to get out there and birdwatch. Birds are there for us all. Most of all … enjoy yourself!

PART 1

Chapter 1

Ireland — A Birdwatching Paradise

Dipper *(Joe Curtis)*

In recent years, Ireland has become the destination of a new breed of tourist: the birdwatcher. The reasons are very easy to understand. Ireland has some of the largest breeding seabird colonies in the world, has huge flocks of wintering shorebirds and wildfowl (ducks and geese) and the best autumn seabird migration of any location in Europe. In spring and autumn, there is also the possibility of seeing a host of rare and unusual migrant species. The other great

The Jay is one of three distinct Irish subspecies
(Eddie Dunne)

attraction for birdwatchers is the ease with which many birds can be seen. In summer, a stroll along Howth Head in Dublin or the Cliffs of Moher in Clare will be rewarded with a spectacular variety of seabirds, while in winter our tidal estuaries are crammed with shorebirds and ducks.

There have been up to 430 different species of bird recorded in Ireland. While this may seem a large number, it is only about 4 per cent of the world's entire species of bird. Most scientists consider there to be approximately 10,000–10,500 species in the world, of which approximately 40 per cent are found in South America (the Neotropics).

The world is divided into different zoogeographical regions. Ireland lies within a region known as the Palearctic, which includes Iceland, all of Europe and Asia north of the Himalayas, northern China and mainland Japan. The southern boundary extends from Morocco across the northern Sahara into Arabia and Iran and along the southern boundaries of Tibet and the Gobi Desert. Within this enormous area, the region encompassing all of Europe, Iceland, North Africa and parts of the Middle East is known as the Western Palearctic.

Within a European context, Ireland is unique in that, by comparison to most European countries, it has been isolated as an island for approximately 8,000 years. As a result, Ireland has three distinct subspecies of breeding bird: Coal Tit, Jay and Dipper; the Irish

The Blasket Islands in Kerry — home to tens of thousands of seabirds each summer *(Michael O'Clery)*

Red Grouse is also considered by some to be distinct from those found elsewhere in Europe. In addition, the Shannon Callows of the midland counties and Tory Island in Donegal are among the last strongholds of the globally threatened Corncrake. Dublin and Wexford also hold large breeding populations of the rare and exquisite Roseate Tern (a 'must-see' species for anyone in summer).

The number of species we have in Ireland is dictated by several factors. First, being an isolated island for so long, many non-migratory species have not managed to cross the Irish Sea. This explains why Tawny Owls and Nuthatches do not occur in Ireland. Secondly, when it comes to good breeding sites, many migratory species are at a disadvantage to our resident species. Due to our relatively mild winters, most of our resident species enjoy a low mortality rate and occupy the best nest sites in the best habitats long before the first of the summer migrants arrives. Finally, many migrants (especially birds of prey) do not like to fly over large expanses of open water — a journey all migrants must undertake in order to reach Ireland.

Of the 430 species recorded, approximately 100 are regarded as resident birds (that is, they are found in Ireland all year round). Up to 85 are either summer or winter visitors (such as Swallows and Brent Geese, respectively), while another 30 are passage migrants,

Nuthatch (left) and Tawny Owl are non-migratory, and never reached Ireland after the last Ice Age *(Both photos: Adrian Dancy)*

10

Mild winters in Ireland mean our wetland areas remain largely unfrozen, and thus accessible to feeding birds *(Tom Cuffe)*

using Ireland merely as a stopover on their migration route (such as Whimbrels, Curlew Sandpipers and Little Stints). The other species seen in Ireland are scarce, rare or extremely rare migrants or vagrants blown off course by strong winds and storms. So, depending on how active you choose to be, it's possible to see over 200 species in a single year in Ireland.

Being an island, it is our coastline that provides excellent birdwatching opportunities. Shaped by the erosive power of the sea, the rugged Irish coastline varies from the low, rocky shorelines of the east coast to the high cliffs of the headlands and islands of the southern and western regions. It is along the craggy western and southern coasts that enormous seabird colonies can be found in summer. Birds like Razorbills, Guillemots and Kittiwakes nest on the steepest cliffs, while the islands off Kerry play host to the largest breeding numbers of Storm Petrels in the world. The dramatic Skellig Islands are home to over 28,000 pairs of Gannets, and the brightly coloured Puffins there seem totally unconcerned by human visitors. Ireland's westerly location has also made it one of the best countries in Europe to observe the migration of seabirds in autumn. Sites like Cape Clear Island in Cork, the Bridges of Ross in Clare and Kilcummin Head in Mayo have become Meccas for seabird enthusiasts as thousands of shearwaters,

Whimbrels are long-distance migrants *(Sean Cronin)*

Little Stint — an autumn migrant *(Anthony McGeehan)*

The North Slob in Wexford is one of the outstanding wetland sites in the country *(Sean Cronin)*

petrels and skuas can be seen in favourable conditions. Those interested in gulls have also flocked to Ireland in winter because fishing ports such as Killybegs in Donegal attract rare species from the Arctic regions, while Nimmo's Pier in Galway has made that city the gull capital of Ireland.

Every year, in spring and autumn, millions of birds are migrating. Birds like Swallows are journeying to and arriving from far-off destinations, like southern Africa. Smaller birds, such as Robins, may take shorter flights to and from the Mediterranean Basin. Other long-distance migrants include shorebirds that are flying to and from northern Europe and the Arctic tundra. Many species are simply stopping off in Ireland en route to other destinations. Known as passage migrants, most of these 'transit' visitors are shorebirds, but also include the many seabirds that pass off our coastlines on their way to wintering areas in the South Atlantic.

Ireland also has extensive areas of wetlands, with lakes, marshes and tidal estuaries attracting thousands of birds each winter. For example, the mudflats of the North Bull Island in Dublin hold over 20,000 shorebirds each winter, including Black and Bar-tailed Godwits, Knot and Dunlin. Feeding alongside them are Brent Geese and various ducks, including Teal,

Wigeon, Pintail, Shoveler and Shelduck. To have such a variety of birdlife within a European capital city is unique. Further south, the Wexford Wildfowl Reserve holds half the world's population of Greenland White-fronted Geese and large numbers of Whooper Swans, while the more remote islands and coastal grasslands in western and north-western regions attract large skeins of Barnacle Geese. The many wetland areas surrounding Lough Neagh in Northern Ireland attract large numbers of wildfowl, while each winter the Lough itself holds one of the largest concentrations of diving ducks found in Europe.

Its location on the western edge of Europe means Ireland is ideally located to attract such birds. Dominated by the mild Atlantic weather systems, our climate rarely suffers the harsh winter weather that grips our European neighbours each year. Our comparatively mild winters provide rich, soft feeding for thousands of waders, while our wet climate creates the necessary wetlands for countless wildfowl. As well as that, our relatively snow-free weather provides ideal wintering grounds for migrant thrushes and finches, and our resident species.

Whooper Swans travel from Iceland to spend the winter in Ireland *(Annette Cutts)*

Ireland's hedgerows are full of birds *(Michael O'Clery)*

Ireland's hedgerows are another unique feature of our countryside. The thousands of kilometres of hedgerows provide food, cover and nesting sites for many resident species, such as Wrens, Robins, Dunnocks and Blackbirds, as well as for summer migrants like Whitethroats and Chiffchaffs. In more western counties, the repetitive call of the Cuckoo is the harbinger of summer, while the first Swallow of the year is noted in all the national newspapers. In our woodlands, the summer dawn chorus is a cacophony of sound with the musical songs of thrushes, warblers, Robins and Wrens. Blackcaps, a summer visitor to our shores, have become more common in recent years and their beautiful melodies add a touch of class to the symphony. Our hedgerows and woodlands can appear very quiet in late autumn and winter, but this isn't so. Mistle Thrushes and Song Thrushes clear bushes and trees clean of their berries by early winter, while roving flocks of Siskins, Redpolls and Blue, Great, Coal and Long-tailed Tits patrol the upper canopies of the woodland treetops. In gardens, Robins, Dunnocks, Chaffinches and Blackbirds feed on open lawns. A bird table or nut-feeders will attract an eager selection of hungry visitors, like Greenfinches and Goldfinches.

Ireland holds one last superb attraction for the birdwatcher — solitude. Birdwatching is still in its youth in Ireland and it's not unusual to spend a mid-week day at one of Europe's hotspots, in perfect weather conditions, at the right time of the year, and not meet another soul. The opportunity of finding your own birds is unsurpassed. Ireland is uncrowded and, combined with beautiful, unspoilt scenery, makes for exciting and unforgettable birdwatching experiences.

Blue Tits are one of Ireland's commonest birds
(Sean Cronin)

14

Chapter 2

The Wonderful World of Feathers

Gannet *(Clive Timmons)*

Have you ever wondered what makes a bird, a bird? It's a question I love to ask and the answer is quite simple: feathers. Birds are the only creatures in the world that have feathers.

For me, feathers are everything because they allow me to identify birds. Without the subtle differences in colour and tone, wing length and shape, I simply would not have an idea what I am looking at. Imagine, if you possibly can, a Goldfinch, a Brambling and a Chaffinch perched naked before us. If they did not have feathers, we could not really tell one from the other nor, more importantly, could they tell one another apart. Put feathers back on them and behold the golden wings and red face of the Goldfinch, the orange on the wings and breast of a Brambling, and the brick-red breast and steel-blue head of the Chaffinch. As a birdwatcher, feathers are the all-consuming subject of my interest. Without them, birds have no meaning, no beauty and no 'personality'. I can spend hours lost in the contours,

Goldfinch *(Sean Cronin)*, Brambling *(Eddie Dunne)* and Chaffinch *(Joe Curtis)*. They all look very different, but would it be so easy were it not for their feathers?

colours and patterns of feathers, noting the differences of one from the other, ageing and sexing the bird based on the patterns I see and identifying each bird on a combination of the features those patterns reveal. Simple feathers can render hardened birdwatchers speechless when they reveal a splash of red as a Black Redstart takes flight, or when a male Goldcrest raises its brilliant orange-red crown feathers.

Of course, feathers aren't on birds merely for our aesthetic pleasure. Nor do they exist to allow birds to be categorised into those neat, scientific groupings required by humans to make sense of what we see. Feathers are an evolutionary stroke of genius that allow birds to fly, to display and to keep warm and dry. Feathers have enabled birds to conquer every continent, to breed in the harshest climates from the Antarctic to the hottest deserts, to travel thousands of kilometres each year, to remain camouflaged when danger threatens, to dive in the oceans, and to fly over the highest mountains. Feathers are everything!

There are three different types of feather on birds. The first are the soft, down feathers that are closest to the skin and effectively keep the bird warm. Birds live constantly surrounded by this 'duvet' of feathers (every day is a 'duvet day'). When you think about it, they need these feathers in order to survive the cold winter nights or the harsh conditions at sea. Young birds are usually naked when they hatch and the first feathers they grow are soft, downy ones because they don't need to do

A Robin in typical pose, feathers sleeked down on a warm afternoon *(Clive Timmons)*

anything but keep warm. Young water birds, on the other hand, have a complete set of downy feathers when they hatch because they usually leave the nest immediately and take to the water when barely an hour old. In fact, birds like ducks possess more warm, insulating down than any other group of birds. Hence we harvest the down from female Eider ducks. This down, which the female ducks pluck from their own breasts in order to line their nests, is considered to be one of the warmest naturally produced insulations in the world. The 'down harvest' is done without harming the birds at all; each nest has an abundance of down feathers.

The second group of feathers is known as contour feathers. These cover all the external areas of the bird. Contour feathers overlap one another to provide water- and wind-proofing as well as stream-lining the bird for flight. Have you ever noticed that birds always roost (sleep) facing into the wind? This keeps the contour feathers against the body; if they faced tail to the wind, the feathers would be ruffled and the insulation breached. A bird's temperature can also be regulated by fluffing up these feathers to trap air in cold conditions: this explains why birds in your garden always look rounded, fat and 'fluffy' in the snow. Alternatively, in warm weather the body temperature is cooled down by pressing the feathers tightly against the body, giving the bird a lovely sleek appearance. It always amazes me how different a common Irish bird can look when seen in a hot country (another complication for the identification process).

This Robin has fluffed up its body feathers to help insulate against the cold *(Adrian Dancy)*

The last group of feathers is the most important one for many species — the flight feathers or, to give them their correct name, remiges (a good word to add to your 'words to impress' list). These, along with the tail feathers (rectrices), are the longest and most hardwearing. Flight feathers comprise two main groups: the secondaries and the all-important primaries, of which there are usually ten, arranged from the tip of the wing inwards. Without primary feathers, a bird simply could not get airborne, which explains why most wildfowl in collections are pinioned (the primaries are cut) to prevent them from flying off.

Many species also have a 'preen gland' near the base of their tails which produces an oil that the bird preens into its plumage to provide further waterproof sealing. In some seabirds, it is this resin that keeps them buoyant. Other species, like herons and parrots, produce talc from 'powder-down' feathers. These special feathers fray at the tip as they grow and produce a powdery talc that is preened into the plumage to provide a shine and also to assist with waterproofing.

Feathers are extremely light (hence the saying, 'as light as a feather'). Have you ever woken up in the morning and thought that your nails felt heavy?

This Mallard is using a preen gland near its tail to waterproof the feathers with a special oil *(Michael Finn)*

I'm sure you haven't because your nails are made of a lightweight substance called keratin. Most times, you are not even aware of them at the end of your fingers and toes. Feathers are made primarily of the same substance and, just like your nails, are both extremely light and very strong. Given the fact that a bird's propulsion depends almost entirely on its flight feathers, these are the strongest set. Looking more closely at a flight feather reveals the secret of its strength and lightness. The long, central shaft is hollow, with vanes extending outwards and held together by a complicated pattern of interlocking barbs and filaments. These are hooked together in much the same manner as a 'zipper'. Should any of the vanes become separated from one other, they can be 're-zipped' when a bird preens. By running their bills lengthways along each feather, birds close any gaps or breaks in them, ensuring that they are in perfect condition for flight and insulation. For that reason, birds spend long periods of time each day preening all their feathers back into shape — their life depends on it.

There is one major problem with feathers, however. Unlike our nails, feathers do not grow continuously. Once a feather has grown, it is effectively dead. Over the course of time, they become worn and damaged. This reduces a feather's ability to provide waterproofing or adequate strength for flight. For that reason, feathers are moulted (replaced) annually. Growing new feathers is a slow and energy-consuming process, so a moult is undertaken over several weeks (even months), with old feathers gradually being replaced by new ones. This gradual replacement of feathers is an important evolutionary development because most birds need to retain the power of flight when moulting (geese and ducks being the exception to this). Considering the vast distances travelled by many migratory species, it's not surprising that birds need their feathers to be in prime condition for such long-haul flights. Feathers can get very damaged in summer when birds are going in and out of nests feeding their young, so the best time for such a moult is immediately after the breeding season. This is called the post-nuptial moult (a lovely term, don't you

Here we can see how the brown hood of a summer-plumaged Black-headed Gull is gradually replaced by white winter feathers, except for a small, dark spot behind the eye *(Top and middle: Sean Cronin. Bottom: Anthony McGeehan)*

think?), during which time many birds grow a new set of body and wing feathers. This moult gives migratory birds a completely fresh set of flight feathers before setting off on their migrations, while non-migratory birds have a new set of insulating feathers to see them through the cold winter months ahead.

This young Grey Heron is drying its wings after preening. Good feather care is a matter of life and death to a bird *(Joe Curtis)*

Regular preening keeps this Linnet's wing feathers in tip-top condition *(Anthony McGeehan)*

Many species also go through a partial moult on their wintering grounds, before their return spring migration flight. During these partial moults, they usually replace head, body and some wing feathers, but never the important flight feathers. This spring moult gives birds their 'summer plumage' and explains why migrants arriving on our shores in spring are usually in immaculate condition. Not all birds acquire their summer plumage through moult, though. Birds like Linnets, Stonechats and Reed Buntings actually reach this stage when the tips of their head and body feathers wear away to reveal the brighter colours that lie underneath. But these are the exceptions rather than the rule.

Summer plumage is extremely important because it allows males to display their prowess to potential mates. These displays of colour act as ways of telling females that the male is healthy and strong, making him a perfect provider for a family and a worthy protector of the breeding territory. Colour plays such an important role that it's not unknown for a male Robin to attack a ball of red wool left in his area. What peahen could not but be impressed by the long tail feathers of a displaying Peacock in summer? In fact, one of the greatest disappointments in my birdwatching travels was seeing male Peacocks in their dull, tail-less winter plumage in India. In the world of birds, it is often the male that is more colourful and attractive than the female (unlike us humans, I hasten to add!). For many species, the female wears the dull browns and boring greys, while the males are the flamboyant ones in their blues, greens and reds. There is a very good reason for this. Where the female is the duller of the two, it's usually she who takes on the role of incubating the eggs and sitting on the chicks to keep them warm. If the colourful male were to sit on a reasonably exposed nest, any passing predator would see him instantly. When a species nests in holes or under cover, the need for the female to be well camouflaged is reduced and both birds tend to look very similar. For that reason, both male and female Kingfishers are beautifully adorned with blues and oranges.

I can't leave this subject without mentioning a very special group of wading birds called phalaropes.

The superb camouflage of a Sandwich Tern chick *(Anthony McGeehan)*

In this group, the roles are totally reversed, with females being brightly coloured and males being comparatively dull. The poor male holds the territory, builds the nest and, once the female has laid the eggs, does all the incubation. While the male is left looking after the chicks, the female does not assist in any way in their upbringing and will often go off and mate with other males (dreadfully unfair … don't you think?). For many ground-nesting birds, their summer plumage has evolved to serve as camouflage during their breeding season. Wading birds such as godwits are grey and white in winter, which helps them to blend into the greyness of the mudflats. In summer, a godwit's plumage is transformed into bright chestnut underparts and dappled black and red upperparts — perfect for disappearing into the high Arctic tundra, where they breed. Young wading birds, and many seabirds such as terns and gulls, also rely on camouflage. Not being able to fly, their only defence is to keep still or lie low. So good is this camouflage that they can simply blend into the grass or shingle without a trace.

When a young bird fledges (leaves the nest), it will have a complete set of wing and tail feathers but usually 'juvenile' head and body feathers that, in most, are moulted very quickly in time for their first winter. In small birds, this first-winter plumage is essentially the same as that of an adult, but will usually show pale tips to some of the wing feathers. By the following spring, another partial moult produces an adult plumage. Usually the bigger the bird, the longer it takes for it to become a full adult. In medium-sized species, it may take two years before reaching adulthood, while in larger birds, like gulls for example, it may take four or five years. As they grow older and each time they moult, a new plumage emerges, and an understanding of each plumage phase allows us to age each bird accurately. Hence we often refer to individual birds as a second-winter or a third-summer etc. However, once they reach their full adult plumage it becomes almost impossible to age them. A ten-year-old bird looks exactly the same as a 40-year-old bird because each year they grow a brand new set of pristine feathers. It would be like us turning 18 and, at the end of each

This Mute Swan cygnet will have 25,000 feathers by the time it is fully grown (Annette Cutts)

summer, shedding our skin to reveal a fresh 18-year-old complexion again … no need for anti-wrinkle creams!

While it may appear that we understand everything there is to know about birds' feathers and plumage moults, I know from experience that there are some strange happenings in the world of feathers. Why, for example, was a Wandering Albatross caught in Australian waters some years ago still essentially in a juvenile plumage when the ring on its legs revealed it to be some ten years old? No one knows the answer, which is a good thing in my opinion — it's one more question for us to ponder.

Talking of pondering, I'll end as I began, with another question. Have you ever wondered how many feathers a bird actually has? Needless to say, the bigger the bird, the more feathers it will have. A Mute Swan can have as many as 25,000 individual contour feathers (I have often wondered, who counted them?). Very small birds, like hummingbirds, can have as little as 100 individual feathers. Regardless of the quantity, the evolution of feathers has allowed birds to develop into the many wonderful varieties that surround us today.

Can you imagine a world without birds? Without feathers, birds aren't birds … feathers are everything indeed.

Chapter 3

Beaks Galore

Shag *(Clive Timmons)*

Perhaps the single most important and revolutionary theory ever to emerge from the scientific world stemmed from a simple observation about the beak of a bird. I'm referring to Charles Darwin and his observations on specimens of finches 'collected' from different islands of the Galapagos. All the birds were superficially the same, except for one thing: the size of their beaks. It seemed that each type had adapted to its specific surroundings on the different islands and, over time, had formed unique species. With this simple observation, the complex theory of evolution was crystallised; recent work carried out on 'Darwin's Finches' by Peter Grant has shown that these very same birds are still applying such adaptations today.

In my travels around the world, I've seen over 2,500 species of birds. From treecreepers to toucans, herons to hummingbirds, I'm constantly astounded by the form and variety of beak sizes and shapes I encounter. While you should never judge a book by its cover, you can certainly judge a bird by its beak. Beaks tell you so many things: what the bird feeds on, where it feeds and how it feeds. So, what's in a beak?

Treecreepers have a fine, curved bill for extracting small insects from tree bark *(John Fox)*

Grey Herons have a large, dagger-like bill, particularly well suited to catching fish *(Joe Curtis)*

Costa's Hummingbirds have a specially adapted, needle-like bill for sipping nectar from flowers *(Eric Dempsey)*

In order to fly, birds have evolved several adaptations, including a lightweight bone structure and aerodynamic wings. A mouthful of teeth would also be a serious burden for flight and certainly make the bird front-heavy. Instead, birds have beaks (or bills) made of keratin. Of course, such an instrument means that a bird can't chew or bite like mammals or reptiles can. In fact, most beak movements are restricted to simple up-and-down, open-and-close actions with only the lower section (the lower mandible) hinged and movable. Despite these restrictions, birds have developed to take advantage of many different food sources, and their beak shapes and sizes have evolved to adapt to every conceivable niche available in the natural world.

Look at finches in an Irish garden. Their beaks are conical (cone-shaped). Straightaway this is a sign that they are primarily seed-eaters. The conical beak is ideal for holding and cracking hard seed cases. However, if all finch beaks were the same, the birds would be limited to the same food source and competition would be high. Therefore it makes sense for different finches to utilise different food sources. For that reason, Greenfinches have thick beaks, which are perfect for cracking harder and tougher seeds than those tackled by Chaffinches. By comparison, Goldfinches have thinner and more pointed beaks, perfect for extracting seeds from thistles and teasels. Perhaps the most unusual finch beak is that of the Crossbill. Similar in size and shape to the Greenfinch, Crossbills have evolved a unique bill where, as the name suggests, the upper and lower mandibles are actually crossed. This extraordinary bill is perfect for prising apart pine cones, which are their only food source. With a sidewards movement (itself unique in the bird world), Crossbills can open the seed heads and extract the soft seed inside using either their upper mandible or their tongues. On the down side, this unique bill means they can't pick up seeds from the ground like other finches.

Now, compare the bills of birds like Robins, wagtails and pipits to those of the finches. It immediately becomes obvious that they have long, thin and pointed bills. These are the classic beaks of the insect-eaters. A pointed bill allows a bird to pick insects from under leaves, off a road or pluck them from the air. It is as precise an instrument as your index finger and thumb. Of course, such birds are not totally reliant on insects and can change to different food items in winter. They cannot tackle hard seeds or nuts like the finches can, however, which is why you don't find them on the feeders in your garden. Treecreepers are also insect-eaters, but their long, pointed bill is down-curved, making it ideal for searching for earwigs and larvae in the barks of trees. Bee-eaters also have slightly decurved, pointed bills that allow them not only to catch bees but to expertly remove the sting before swallowing the disarmed

Greenfinches have a larger bill than Chaffinches and Goldfinches, better for tackling larger nuts *(Joe Curtis)*

Chaffinches have fine, conical bills, ideal for small nuts and seeds *(Clive Timmons)*

Goldfinches, like the Chaffinch, have a fine, pointed bill, perfect for extracting seeds from thistles *(Joe Curtis)*

Crossbills are the only species which has a 'crossed' bill — used to extract seeds from pine cones *(Anthony McGeehan)*

Robins have a classic insect-eater's bill — fine and pointed, ideal for grabbing small, fast-moving prey *(Tom Cuffe)*

Pied Wagtails — their thin, pincer-like bill is ideal for catching insects *(Adrian Dancy)*

Rock Pipits are shoreline specialists. Their slightly larger bill allows them to take larger insects *(Adrian Dancy)*

The agile Bee-eater can catch bees and other large insects in flight *(Anthony McGeehan)*

insect. Other pointed bills are used for catching fish in much the same way. While birds adopt different methods for catching fish, the beak shape remains consistent. In effect, terns, herons, gannets, grebes and kingfishers all have the same dagger-like bill. Birds of prey have evolved hooked bills that are perfect for tearing flesh, while halfway along the upper mandible most have a pointed 'tooth' used for dispatching prey.

It is only when you enter an ecosystem that is crammed full of birds that the different bill adaptations really become obvious. Among the thousands of wading birds feeding on a mudflat, for example, all shapes and sizes of bills can be seen side by side. The Curlew has a long, decurved bill that it uses to delve deep into the mud in search of molluscs and lugworms. Alongside might be a Dunlin, using the same method, but with a considerably shorter bill. Waders probe into the mud and use the sensitive tips to their bills to find their food. However, neither the Curlew nor the Dunlin is competing with each other as the length of their respective bills determines the depth into the mud that each wader can search for food. The Curlew, having the longer bill, is probing much deeper into the layer of mud than is the Dunlin.

All birds of prey, such as this Buzzard, have strongly hooked bills for tearing meat *(Joe Curtis)*

Oystercatcher

Black-tailed Godwit

Curlew

Greenshank

Snipe

Lapwing

Redshank

Avocet

Curlew Sandpiper

Ringed Plover

Little Stint

Curlew *(Anthony McGeehan)*, Black-tailed Godwit *(Clive Timmons)*, Oystercatcher *(Eric Dempsey)*, Greenshank *(Eric Dempsey)*, Snipe *(Eric Dempsey)*, Redshank *(Annette Cutts)*, Curlew Sandpiper *(Tom Cuffe)*, Ringed Plover *(Anthony McGeehan)*, Little Stint *(Adrian Dancy)*, Avocet *(Adrian Dancy)*, Lapwing *(Clive Timmons)*, Background image *(Tom Cuffe)*

Along the shore, another highly evolved wader, the Turnstone, uses its short, wedge-shaped and slightly upturned bill to flick over small rocks or clumps of seaweed in search of small shrimps and insects.

Even birds of the same species have adopted different techniques. As the tide drops, Oystercatchers begin feeding on the mudflats. Their long bills are ideal for catching worms. However, Oystercatchers also have a liking for molluscs, which must first be extracted from their shells. There are two different schools of teaching among Oystercatchers: the smashers and the prisers. Prising a mollusc from its shell requires great skill. More importantly, it also requires the bird to have a pointed bill. Therefore Oystercatchers with pointed bills are always mollusc-prisers. On the other hand, those in the smashing fraternity end up with blunt-tipped bills as a result of their actions; they are never mollusc-prisers. Young Oystercatchers learn their techniques from their parents, and I often wonder how many confused, young birds might be out there whose parents are graduates of the two different schools.

Other birds have developed even stranger methods for feeding and as a result have very unusual bill shapes. Spoonbills have long, spatulate-shaped bills. Placing their bill into the water, they feed with sideways movements of the head, filtering out tiny crustaceans and fish as they move along. Avocets use a similar sweeping movement, holding their long, upturned bill slightly open as they feed. The highly sensitive bill then snaps shut on any worm or other invertebrate it feels. Of course, some water birds have brought their beak shapes to the extreme and there is no better example than the Pelicans. Their bills act like giant fishing nets. The birds scoop up as many fish as possible in the bottom, baggy part of the bill. Before swallowing their catch, they must open their beaks slightly and squeeze out the water, leaving their

Oystercatcher — smasher or priser? *(Adrian Dancy)*

rich catch inside. Skimmers, a species of tern found in America, Asia and Africa, are even more unusual. These birds' lower mandibles are longer than the upper and they feed by flying very low over the water and opening their bills. The lower mandible is placed under the water and creates a furrow as the birds flies. When it encounters a fish, the lower mandible slams shut and the prey is caught.

It is perhaps in the Tropics that bill shapes and forms reach their greatest variety. In these lush environments, many species have entered into a relationship with specific plant species. These symbiotic relationships (as they are known) mean that both plant and bird gain from the affiliation. In many ways, they cannot exist without each other and have evolved to meet each other's needs. The plant offers rich nectar or fruit, while the bird acts as a pollinator (carrying pollen on its head or body as it moves from plant to plant) or disperses the seeds in its droppings.

On some occasions, plants can depend on just one species of bird as a pollinator or seed-disperser.

The ways in which birds seek nectar from flowers varies greatly. In Australia, some parrots and lorrikeets have special hairs on the tongue for licking up the nectar. On the same continent, honeyeaters use their long, curved bills to extract the nectar, and in Africa the same technique is employed by sunbirds. However, one group of birds has perfected the art of nectar-feeding to such an extent that they have evolved the longest bills per body size of any species. Found on the American continent, hummingbirds are among the most specialised birds in the world and are found in every habitat from Alaska to the High Andes and the lush Central American tropical rainforests. Moving from flower to flower, they drink nectar using their long, bi-forked tongues — very much like a proboscis of an insect. Some species have evolved extremely long, sometimes decurved bills that allow

The extraordinary bill of the Spoonbill is used to sift through mud and silt for food *(Sean Cronin)*

The Avocet uses its thin, upcurved bill to take tiny items of food from the upper layer of mudflats *(Adrian Dancy)*

Puffins lose the brightly coloured plates on their bills in winter *(Clive Timmons)*

Red spots at the tip of this Herring Gull's bill stimulate their chicks to beg for food *(Mícheál Casey)*

them to feed from the long, tubed, nectar-rich flowers. It is remarkable when you compare the shape of the bills of these birds to the shape of the flowers they feed from — they are both identical and perfectly suited to one another. The medium- to shorter-billed species are more opportunistic and feed on a variety of flowers as well as on flies and gnats. These latter hummingbirds are usually not in a symbiotic relationship with plants, while the larger-billed birds tend to feed from a very small variety of flowers, with some relying on one species alone. For that reason, many of these plants are in flower all year round.

Besides feeding, beaks have other important roles. In order to keep their precious feathers well conditioned for flight and for insulation, birds need to preen and they use their beaks to do so (except for one species, the Sword-billed Hummingbird, which has a bill measuring more than half its body length, making it too long for preening). Mutual preening is also vital during courtship, serving to strengthen the bonds

between pairs. Bill colour plays an important role for many birds, too, particularly for display and threat. Puffins, for example, have their brightly coloured bills only for the summer months before shedding the outer plates for the winter. Many bird beaks change colour in summer and form part of the courtship displays in the lead-up to the breeding season. Bill colour can also stimulate the chick to beg for food, with large gulls having bright red spots on the lower mandible for that very reason.

Finally, looking at the mastery of bird nests, it's sometimes hard to believe that such incredible creations are made not by the hands of a master craftsman, but by the beak of a bird. To wonder at the delicate weaving of grass, hair and cobwebs in most Irish nests is to appreciate how sensitive, delicate and wonderfully creative and useful beaks actually are. As a person who can't hammer a nail into the wall, it makes me sort of envious … waiter, may I have a bill, please?

Chapter 4

Epic Journeys — Spring Migration

Wheatear *(John Finn)*

Spring is one of the most exciting times of the year for birdwatchers. A close friend of mine believes that every single spring migrant returning to our shores deserves to be met with a full orchestra playing to maximum strength in celebration of their remarkable journey. When I see my first migrant each year, I cannot help but be acutely aware of the changing seasons and of the passage of time. I believe that even those who have little interest in the natural world notice the first arrival of summer birds.

It was the Greek philosopher Aristotle who once wrote that 'one Swallow does not a summer make', and given recent Irish summers, never was a truer word spoken. If one bird were to epitomise the change of seasons, the Swallow is it. They have been the heralds of spring and a promise of long summer days for people in the northern hemisphere for thousands of years. Perhaps they stir within us a primal instinct, a subconscious anticipation of the approaching time of plenty that dates right back to our ancestors. In all

Swallow *(Anthony McGeehan)*

cultures, from Asia and Europe to North America, Swallows are considered to bring good fortune to those lucky enough to have them nesting near their homes. References to the Swallows' arrival have been found on inscriptions on ancient Greek vases, in the Bible and in the first-century writings of the Roman naval commander and naturalist, Pliny. Even today, ask anyone to name a migrant bird and most people will say, 'the Swallow'.

I sometimes wonder what Aristotle would make of the arrival dates of the first Swallows into Ireland these days. In recent years, some have been seen here four to five weeks earlier than we would expect for the first of our spring migrants. Until 1990, the earliest Swallow ever seen in Ireland was the first week of March. Since then, birds have been recorded as early as the first week of February. In 2004, some early arrivals even brought a much rarer Mediterranean cousin with them, a Red-rumped Swallow. So what are these summer migrants doing here so early, and could they have flown all the way from southern Africa and reached our shores by February?

The truth is fascinating. These birds haven't actually flown that far in migratory terms. Over the last 15 years, thousands of Swallows and martins have started to remain in the Mediterranean Basin. While such species have wintered in small numbers in this region in the past, the fact that such a large population is now choosing to do so marks a significant change in their behaviour. Why this has occurred is still not known — is it an effect of global warming, or are there other factors at work? One logical suggestion may be that the birds are enjoying very late summers (our so-called Indian summers). This extends the breeding season for birds like Swallows, allowing them an opportunity to raise a third and even a fourth brood. By the end of September, these late broods may still be at the nest when many other Swallows are

Sand Martin *(Anthony McGeehan)*

already well on their way towards South Africa. By the time they are fledged, it's simply too late for them to undertake such a journey, so they winter in the Mediterranean instead.

Whatever the reason, it appears that these birds are now finding enough food over the marshes and wetlands in Spain to sustain them through the northern winter. Some Swallows have even become resident in Spain. Conditions there must now be good enough for these birds to consider it more beneficial to stay in Spain rather than to make the extremely dangerous journeys that other migrants take on twice a year.

An understanding of the migration of birds is a relatively recent development. Gilbert White, writing in *The Natural History and Antiquities of Selbourne* in 1788, reached the conclusion that Swallows spend the winter hibernating in mud at the bottom of ponds and lakes. This theory was shared by most eminent naturalists of the day and stemmed from the fact that

in autumn, Swallows were usually seen hawking insects over ponds and lakes during the day before roosting in reedbeds at night. Then, overnight, they would seem to disappear for the winter. In the spring, the first birds would again be seen feeding over these wetland areas.

While this seems to be a rather fanciful explanation as to how migrants suddenly appear each spring, the truth is equally unbelievable. The first wave of spring migrants begins to arrive in Ireland from mid-March onwards, with the main influx from mid-April. For many, their journey starts in early February when they begin to leave their wintering quarters in South Africa. Many feed as they go; others store up fat reserves and attempt to travel long distances without needing to stop for food. Many travel north over the Namib and Kalahari Deserts up to the Gulf of Guinea. Here many birds turn inland and reach the southern edges of the Sahara by early

Cape Clear Island in Cork — one of the first landfalls for many tired migrants *(Joe Curtis)*

March. This is perhaps the most dangerous part of their migration as they face the vast and ever-widening expanse of the arid Sahara. With high temperatures, few feeding opportunities and prevailing northerly winds, many birds die in the effort.

Those that survive reach North Africa in a weakened state, but press on past the Atlas Mountains and over the Mediterranean into Europe. Here they face a different (and mindless) danger as they run the gauntlet of trigger-happy shooters in Portugal, Spain, Italy and Malta. Millions of migrant birds are slaughtered each year, despite European legislation that grants them protection. Irish birds that survive this barrage eventually reach northern France and travel out across the sea to reach southern Ireland. It's a journey of over 9,500 km and is achieved in less than two months.

By comparison, birds wintering in the Mediterranean are much closer to the breeding grounds of northern Europe, requiring a migration of less than 1,500 km to reach Ireland. At the first sign of good weather, these Mediterranean wintering migrants move north, arriving well in advance of the others. Should the weather remain good, they will stay, giving them a headstart in selecting the choice territories, thus increasing their chances of breeding success. It's a high-risk strategy and the gamble doesn't always pay off. As we all know well, Irish weather can be extremely unpredictable in February and March. Should the weather turn bad, these early arrivals are faced with a difficult choice: stay and brave out the weather in hope of maintaining a good territory, or return south, using up vital energy and fat stores. It's not clear what they do in such circumstances, but I would suggest that these birds return south again and await more favourable conditions. By then, of course, the main wave of migrants may already be moving out of Africa.

With so many dangers to face, the big question is: why do birds migrate in the first place? The answer lies in the availability of food. This is the driving force behind all migration. Most summer migrants require a plentiful supply of insects, and each year a largely untapped and almost endless supply of insects is available in Europe. Secondly, in northern Europe the

Some Wheatears migrate from Africa to Greenland and back each year *(Clive Timmons)*

Sandwich Terns winter off West Africa and migrate to nest in northern Europe *(Anthony McGeehan)*

birds enjoy long daylight hours, allowing them to start feeding their young very early in the morning and continue late into the evening. Some birds can be active for up to 15 hours each day in mid-summer (or more, depending on how far north the birds are). As a result, many species manage to raise more than one brood of chicks each summer. These are the paybacks for migrating north in summer. By late autumn, however, this food supply is decreasing and birds need to depart south in order to survive. It has been a natural and spectacular cycle that has been continuing for millennia.

How migrants navigate is still not fully understood by scientists. Many migrant birds weigh little more than 10 grams and have brains no bigger than a pea. Yet they can store migration routes of over 9,500 km and use the sun, stars and familiar landscapes to find their way. It's even believed that migrant birds can store and memorise the unique odours of their breeding grounds and may even be capable of seeing the magnetic fields of the Earth.

Spring migration (or, more correctly, return migration) differs significantly from that of autumn.

Birds have a sense of urgency to return to the breeding grounds, and the spring journey can sometimes take as little as half to two-thirds the time to complete than the outward autumn journey. The returning birds are adults and all have the experience of having completed at least one previous migration. They know the best routes and are familiar with key navigational landmarks. As a result, few spring migrants get lost in the same way as young birds can when migrating for the first time in autumn. Likewise, the European spring weather is usually good, so fewer birds get blown off course as they might on their outward journey. Having said that, weather does play an important role in return migration.

All migrants benefit from a tailwind when flying, and if by mid-March there are light southerly winds, birds such as Wheatears, Sandwich Terns and Sand Martins will be seen along our southern and eastern coastlines. These are traditionally the first group of summer birds to arrive in Ireland and are quickly followed by the first warblers, such as Chiffchaffs and Willow Warblers. Many of these birds may have wintered north of the equator and are moving ahead of

Night Heron, a classic spring overshoot migrant
(Eric Dempsey)

Squacco Heron, another, even rarer one
(Warren Hewitt)

the millions of birds streaming up across the African continent further south. Most migrants are reluctant to cross open water, opting instead to cross at the narrowest land points available. Locations like Gibraltar in Spain, the Bosphorus in Turkey and Eilat in Israel act like funnels through which these birds pass in quite spectacular numbers. Overhead, thousands of White Storks and birds of prey circle in rising columns on the thermals, while every bush and tree seems to be alive with warblers. Over the marshlands, countless numbers of Swallows, Swifts and Bee-eaters are found. Visible migration, as it's known, is an experience of a lifetime. To see thousands of birds fly in off the sea or watch as soaring eagles and buzzards pass overhead is a memory to savour. Once safely through these 'funnels', the birds spread out and northwards across Europe.

Despite the millions of birds that reach Ireland each year, we rarely experience such concentrated mass arrivals. Our birds seem to arrive on a more phased basis. Occasionally, however, low-pressure weather systems just north of the Mediterranean can produce extremely unfavourable migration conditions, sometimes referred to as 'blocking lows'. They aren't called 'blocking lows' for nothing. Such weather systems, especially those with rain on their southern edges or with strong, head-on northerly winds, act like brick walls to migrating birds, forcing them to drop down and seek shelter at the earliest opportunity. The migrants remain where they are, feeding and waiting for a change in the weather. Meanwhile, further south, more birds are arriving, and should the weather remain unchanged for some time, an avian traffic jam is created, with up to 100 million birds all waiting for favourable conditions. When the weather does eventually break, the floodgates are opened and birds move en masse into western and northern Europe. Almost overnight, Swallows are everywhere, Whitethroats and Willow Warblers are singing, and Swifts are wheeling around our towns and cities.

Spotted Flycatcher is one of the latest migrants to arrive each summer, usually in late May *(Adrian Dancy)*

An exotic visitor from the warmer parts of Europe, a few Hoopoes reach Ireland each year *(Sean Cronin)*

For that reason, birdwatchers are constantly watching the weather forecasts throughout the spring. A southerly airstream from the Mediterranean can always result in the arrival of an occasional rare visitor, but should we also be experiencing a 'blocking low' lying over Ireland, then the potential for the arrival of lots of rare birds increases. Should the weather system lie over the southern half of Ireland, then birds moving north over the Bay of Biscay make landfall on southern islands and headlands. Likewise, a high pressure over Scandinavia can create south-easterly winds over Ireland, deflecting birds off course from their European routes. When such weather events occur, areas like the Great Saltee Island in Wexford or Cape Clear Island in Cork can be alive with countless common migrants (as well as some exotic species, such as Hoopoe and Woodchat Shrike). Such occurrences are known as 'falls' (perhaps because it seems that the birds fall from the sky). These falls can be quite dramatic, such as that which took place on 3 May 1994 on Cape Clear when 13 Golden Orioles, almost 50 Turtle Doves, three Night Herons, a Red-rumped Swallow, a Dotterel and hundreds of other migrants arrived overnight.

Rare southern birds can also reach Ireland in an even more unusual way by 'overshoot migration'. Put simply, these birds overshoot their intended destinations and go further north than they intended. This can happen when a big area of high pressure lies over the whole of Europe, creating exceptionally good weather with the same temperature and conditions everywhere. Birds simply don't realise that Ireland isn't part of the Mediterranean and keep flying until they reach here (of course they will soon head south again when they feel the wrath of the real Irish summer). It can also happen if a bird simply fails to shut off its migratory urges and flies too far.

The great thing about birdwatching in spring is that all the birds are usually adults in full breeding plumage. None of those difficult-to-identify juvenile plumages at this time of year! Males are also keen to start singing, and even birds that have drifted well off

Black-winged Stilts are another rare Mediterranean wanderer to Ireland *(Derek Charles)*

Woodchat Shrikes are rare visitors to Ireland, mainly in spring *(Warren Hewitt)*

37

Arctic Terns are one of the greatest migrants of all, commuting between the Arctic and Antarctic oceans *(Anthony McGeehan)*

course can be heard holding territory. A classic example of this was when a Scarlet Rosefinch (a bird of eastern and northern Europe) was found in Mayo some years ago. It was heard singing for several days and, even more remarkably, another male was heard to respond further up the valley. Had a female been in the area, perhaps this species would have bred for the first time in Ireland.

Given immense challenges such as crossing deserts, seas and facing into adverse weather conditions (not to mention the shooters in the Mediterranean), it's amazing that so many birds actually complete their journey. The dangers they face each spring are multiple. I once saw thousands of Swallows landing on roads in Spain, having flown into a northerly head wind all the way across the Mediterranean. They were exhausted. Within minutes of landing, hundreds were killed by traffic. We spent

hours picking weak birds off the road and placing them in shelter. I also remember watching warblers in an olive grove in Eilat, Israel. They had completed one of the most difficult stages of their migration, up along the Red Sea from Africa, and were busy feeding and resting. A White-breasted Kingfisher (a large species, about the size of a Mistle Thrush) caught, killed and ate several birds before our very eyes.

Despite all of these seemingly insurmountable obstacles, migrant birds still reach Ireland safely every year. Each individual bird has made a remarkable flight and has endured its own unique struggles to get here. To watch such a bird fly in off the sea into Ireland is to witness an incredible natural event that has taken place for thousands of years. I always look forward to seeing my very first spring migrant each year. I always ponder the journey it has made … and, in my heart, an orchestra is playing!

PART 1

Chapter 5

Spring Birdwatching

Sedge Warbler *(Anthony McGeehan)*

As a birdwatcher, people always astound me when they pronounce the arrival of spring on the first day of February. Are they mad? The first day of February is still the depths of the winter. In fact, February can be the coldest month of the year and often suffers the worst weather. No, let us get one thing straight — spring certainly does not start in February. The people in the 'Met Office' are a little bit more accurate. Meteorologically, the first day of spring falls on 1 March and I can live with this. Having said that, I

Swallows — establishing pairs is a priority for freshly arrived birds *(Sean Cronin)*

don't consider spring to have arrived officially until the first of our spring migrants have been seen … and that doesn't usually happen in earnest until about mid-March. So, as an Irishman, I would like to propose that St Patrick's Day, which falls on 17 March, be officially recognised as the first day of spring.

Of course, people have different things that define for them the arrival of spring. Perhaps it's the first flush of new buds on our trees, or the first daffodils pushing their heads through the ground. For others it's the lengthening of the day and the bright early mornings. I must confess, the first hint of spring for me is when I hear the garden birds in full song each morning or watch Blue Tits check out the nest-box for the breeding season ahead. But truly, it is seeing the first migrant of the year that heralds the official turning of the year in my mind.

For that reason, I find myself drifting towards the coast as the first weeks of March arrive as it's here that the first of the migrants are usually seen. This makes sense of course because, being an island, birds must fly over the sea in order to reach Ireland. But Ireland has a long coastline, so where is the best location for seeing the first migrants? This really does depend on the weather, but it's worth remembering that in spring, birds are travelling from the south, so most migrants arrive into Ireland along a broad front on the south coast. Many migrant birds fly during the night as it affords them better protection from predators as well as allowing them to feed during daylight hours. As a result, it's often headlands with lighthouses (which are usually positioned farther out to sea than other coastal areas) that attract the first wave of migrants. For a migrant travelling at night, the beam of a lighthouse offers an excellent target to follow. Places like Hook Head in Wexford, Brownstown Head in Waterford, and Cork headlands like the Old Head of Kinsale, Galley Head and Mizen Head are ideal spring migrant watching areas. Better still, offshore islands such as Cape Clear in Cork and the Great Saltee in Wexford

The Old Head of Kinsale in Cork — one of the best places to find spring migrants *(Sean Cronin)*

Sand Martin *(Adrian Dancy)*

A singing Grasshopper Warbler *(Mícheál Casey)*

(which both have lighthouses close by) are excellent locations for seeing the first migrants. These areas regularly record the first spring migrants of the year.

The first birds seen are usually those that have travelled the least distance. Birds like Wheatears, Chiffchaffs and Sand Martins are inevitably the first to arrive. It's no coincidence that these species spend the winter just south of the Sahara. By comparison to species like Spotted Flycatchers and Swallows that winter in South Africa, these birds really do have a headstart when it comes to flying north. Another species that is among the first migrants to be seen is the Sandwich Tern. The main wintering areas for them are the coastal countries of West Africa, a minor return journey when compared to that of Arctic Terns, which winter on the Antarctic seas.

The arrival of spring migrants into Ireland is a staggered one. Birds arrive in 'waves', but if we get sustained periods of good weather with southerly (tail) winds, those waves transform into tidal surges of migrants pouring north. As they arrive, the birds slowly work their way up the coasts and inland. By early April, Wheatears are found on piers, headlands and beaches along the east and west coasts, while Swallows and Sand Martins move away from the coast and are found hunting insects over inland reedbeds and lakes. The northward surge continues until, like a pincer movement, birds like Wheatears are found along all coastal counties, and all inland areas are teeming with new arrivals.

Late March and early April see the arrival of our first warblers. The first birds arrive along the south coast. The wonderful thing about the arrival of our warblers is that they seem to instantly burst into song upon setting foot (wing) in Ireland. It's as if they can't wait to start singing. Chiffchaffs are usually the first warblers to arrive. Irish Chiffchaffs winter from the Mediterranean south to sub-Saharan Africa. The birds that arrive in mid-March most likely have spent the winter in the Mediterranean Basin. Those that arrive later have undoubtedly wintered further south. Following closely behind them are Willow Warblers, which are flying north from countries around the Gulf of Guinea. These birds quickly move inland and by mid-April our woodlands and hedgerows are alive with the sounds of these warblers. At the same time, coastal reedbeds come alive with the songs of Sedge Warblers. By the first week of May, warblers can be found in our woodlands, hedgerows, reedbeds and on the open scrublands, where the reeling calls of Grasshopper Warblers are a true sound of spring.

Other species seem to slip through the coastal regions undetected and arrive suddenly, overnight, on their breeding grounds. Corncrakes are rarely seen in spring on southern headlands and islands. Yet in order to reach their nesting sites, they must have passed through or over the south coast. In the midlands area known as the Shannon Callows (the floodplains of the River Shannon), Corncrakes are usually heard by mid-April. They have a very distinctive, rasping 'crek-crek' call and in early spring are vocal throughout the day. It's at this time that you may see males doing their gliding flight display over their territory. By the end of April, the first birds reach islands off the west and north coasts. Tory Island in Donegal is one of the

best locations for seeing the species. Being very secretive, the high grasslands of the Callows make them difficult to see there, but the grass of Tory Island grows slower in spring, thanks to its more northerly location, so it is usually short when the birds arrive. Tory is one of the few places where Corncrakes can be viewed with ease in spring because they are usually 'head and shoulders' above the grass. Watching these 'chicken-like' birds that seem to prefer to walk rather than fly, it's sometimes difficult to comprehend that, like the Swallows, they too have made journeys of over 9,000 km to reach Ireland.

Some seabirds are also long-distance spring migrants and by mid-March, they begin returning to their traditional nesting areas. Some species, like Guillemots, may have wintered just a few kilometres offshore while others, like Razorbills, are returning

Storm Petrels travel vast distances from their wintering grounds in waters off southern Africa, arriving at their nesting grounds in Ireland and north-west Europe in April *(Michael Davis)*

from waters off the Spanish coast. However, others are returning from much farther away. Most of the Irish population of Manx Shearwaters, for example, spends the winter months in the South Atlantic off the coast of Brazil, while Storm Petrels are returning from the seas off South Africa. So in early spring it's always worth visiting the coastal cliffs and islands to see which of the seabirds are back first. Gannets are known to return to the breeding sites as early as February. Older birds usually repossess the nest they used in previous years, but should they fail to return, younger birds will take it over. In the world of Gannets, there is a strict pecking order and many of the birds seen around the breeding colonies in early spring are young birds hopeful of securing a good nest site.

For many of us, migrants are birds like Swallows or Manx Shearwaters, but any bird that has wintered in one area and is returning to another to breed is, by definition, a true migrant. So species like Meadow Pipits and Skylarks that have wintered along the Irish coasts should also be considered migrants. Depending on the severity of the winter, many may have wintered further south, in the Mediterranean. Regardless, by April these birds are beginning to return to the mountains and moorlands to breed. Their aerial flight songs are as much an indicator of the changing year as any returning Swallow. The upland regions also see a return of birds of prey, like Merlins, Peregrine Falcons and Hen Harriers. Wintering on lower moorlands and coastal marshes, they begin to move into their higher altitude breeding grounds by mid-March. In fact, early April is one of the best times to observe raptors, when the males perform their slow, but graceful, aerial displays over their territories. Males will often catch

Meadow Pipits have a complex migration, some moving from lowlands to mountains in spring. Some have wintered in the Mediterranean and others migrate from North Africa to Iceland, passing through Ireland on the way *(Clive Timmons)*

Great Crested Grebe in breeding plumage *(Annette Cutts)*

small items of food. It's as if he is trying to demonstrate to her that he is a good provider … and most times she is impressed.

As May arrives, the last of our summer migrants reach our shores. Cuckoos, Whinchats and Spotted Flycatchers are among the last to arrive. They too waste no time moving inland. Spotted Flycatchers breed in woodlands, and by May the woodlands are alive with insects. There is a golden rule for establishing whether a woodland might be good for birds: if you get eaten alive by insects when you visit, then it's a good woodland! Cuckoos and Whinchats are found in similar habitats ranging from open upland areas to the wetlands of the Shannon Callows.

In spite of all this action and display, for many people who are city- or town-dwellers, like myself, one thing truly marks the arrival of spring — the sound of Swifts. Arriving en masse during the first week of May, the sight and sounds of Swifts wheeling around our town and city skies is the defining moment of the year. These masters of the air have flown almost 10,000 km to get here and their daring aerial chases are a sight to behold. Swifts are, therefore, the true harbingers of spring. The sounds of Cuckoos or Willow Warblers are things that some city-dwellers may only read about, but Swifts in a city … now that is what spring birdwatching is all about!

prey and pass it to the females in elaborate and acrobatic display rituals. By positioning yourself in cover overlooking valleys in the mountains or moorlands, you may just be lucky enough to witness one of the most wonderful spring courtship displays in Ireland.

Having said that, a visit to open lakes and wetlands in April may provide you with an even more elaborate courtship display — that of Great Crested Grebes. By early spring, both males and females are adorned in their full summer plumage of neck and head crests and ruffs. During the courtship display, the male will dive under the water and emerge with a beakful of vegetation. He presents this to the female and the pair perform what can only be described as a dance, which includes head movements and perfectly synchronised swimming. The male will also present

Swift *(Anthony McGeehan)*

Chapter 6

The Language of Birds

Stonechat *(John Finn)*

I believe that the arrival of spring stirs something primal within us humans. It may be something so deep that we may not even be aware of it. For our ancient ancestors, the arrival of spring meant they could look forward to a time of plenty. I wonder if our ancestors stopped and listened to bird song in spring. Did they recognise that as soon as the birds began to sing again, spring had arrived? I ask these questions because hearing the first birds sing in late winter always brings a smile to my face. I know that winter is almost over.

I just love to hear birds singing. I'm not alone. Bird song has uplifted and inspired people down through the ages.

But what is bird song and why do birds sing? Let us be clear from the start, no matter what the poets write: birds don't sing for our pleasure. They sing for three main reasons. First, it's a non-confrontational method of proclaiming ownership of a territory. It's the males that lay claim to and defend territories, so it's usually only the males that sing. I use the word

Blue Tit *(Michael Finn)*

Dunnock *(John Finn)*

Chaffinch *(Michael Finn)*

'usually' because in some species found in the Tropics, females sing quite complex songs. These are often performed as duets with the males during courtship displays, as well as acting as a joint defence of a territory. In fact, it's not unknown for female Robins to sing in winter when trying to defend a territory. In Europe, though, it is the male birds that do most of the singing. No bird wants to risk combat with neighbours, so singing is often enough to deter others from invading their patch.

Secondly, it's a way of attracting a female. Females (being fickle things) find a good song irresistible. A good song means that the male has a territory, which is an essential thing if they are to nest. A territory will provide food and suitable nest sites. The other important signal a good song sends out is that the male is healthy and strong enough to be able to win and hold such a territory, which in turn makes him an ideal partner. The song also allows the females to locate the males — an important thing in a dark

woodland. Once paired, males tend to sing less. Unpaired or widowed males sing more than their paired neighbours.

Thirdly, it's a way for a male bird to inform all of his neighbours that he is still alive. For us, a Wren's song sounds the same ... a Wren is a Wren is a Wren. However, each bird in an area knows the exact song of its neighbours. When one sings, the others listen and then respond with their own songs. Each song is slightly different from the next. By singing at dawn, the birds inform their neighbours that they have survived another night and the status quo remains. However, should one of the birds not sing at dawn, this sends out a very different message. The other birds will very quickly realise that one of the neighbouring males is gone and will immediately invade that territory in order to extend their own.

So, that is why we have what we call a dawn chorus. There are, however, several other good reasons why dawn is the best time to sing. First, it's

A singing Wren — neighbouring Wrens will recognise his song *(John Finn)*

good 'time management'. In the breeding season, most birds are feeding on insects and larvae. In the first glimmer of dawn it is too dark, and perhaps too cool, to find insects. Secondly, sound travels better in cool air. Thirdly, as many migrants fly into Ireland at night, dawn is the best time for the males to attract the attentions of freshly arrived females looking for a mate. The males usually move ahead of females and will have established territories well before the first of the females arrive. Lastly, it's safer to sing at this time because many predators are not very active first thing in the morning. When you think about it, for most of the year small birds spend their time trying to remain as inconspicuous as possible.

Of course, during the breeding season, they behave completely differently. Birds that have spent the winter deep in cover are now to be found sitting on the highest branches or sitting on aerials, singing as loud as they can. They're shouting, 'Here I am!' This is a high-risk strategy. If there's one sure way of

attracting the attentions of a predator, it is sitting out in the open and letting everyone know where you are. Even birds that sing deep in cover are giving away their locations. What is the point in being perfectly camouflaged when you sing? Apparently, birds like Robins and Blackbirds, which proportionally have the largest eyes, are the first to start singing. Having larger eyes makes them more capable of seeing potential danger. It's only as it gets brighter that the other birds risk singing. This explains why the dawn chorus is a staggered event. This period of semi-light is an ideal time to sing. As soon as it gets totally bright, they all gradually stop singing and get on with the business of the day.

The dawn chorus is something everyone should try to experience once in their lives. Standing in a woodland, or in your garden at dawn, and listening to the growing chorus of bird song really is worth getting up early for. For those of us who are not 'morning people', there is always the dusk chorus. In spring and

Robin *(Sean Cronin)*

The cawing of a Rook may not seem like a song to us, but it certainly is to other Rooks *(Joe Curtis)*

summer, birds also sing as day turns to night (for the exact same reasons as they sing at dawn). It doesn't last as long as the dawn chorus (perhaps exhausted adult birds don't want to stay up too long). Like the dawn chorus in reverse, the birds with the largest eyes tend to be last to stop singing at dusk.

Listening to the dawn chorus affords a great opportunity to learn a wide range of bird song (without the background noise of traffic). Being able to recognise different bird songs is great for us, but is vital for birds. They need to be able to distinguish their own species' songs … how else will a female Dunnock be attracted to a male Dunnock? If she were not able to tell a Dunnock from a Robin, then she might find it very difficult to find a mate. Likewise, how could a male know if another male had invaded

his territory? For that reason, bird species have evolved to sing differently. Some songs are extremely complex, while others are simpler. Birds that nest in colonies or loose groups tend to have less complex songs, which explains why the song of a Rook hasn't exactly inspired the poets. But while the raucous notes of a Rook might not be music to our ears, it is, by definition, a true song.

Whether musical or not, a bird's song originates in the syrinx, which consists of paired vocal organs (the syringes). The syringes of all birds have at least one pair of membrane walls that distend into the airstream. Others have more flexible pads that also extend into the airstream. These membranes and pads can be tightened or relaxed by muscles that control the extent to which they vibrate in the airstream, thus

Willow Warblers sing faster if they are occupying good territories *(John Finn)*

Meadow Pipits sing and perform flight displays over their territories *(John Finn)*

creating different sounds. In some species, each of the syringes produces a different sound so that when we hear the song, it is in fact a 'mix' of two distinct songs played as one.

Regardless of the singer, it seems that in most cases the song has to be learned. Young birds listen to songs and begin to learn the phrases as they mature. For example, young male Chaffinches raised early in the summer as part of a first brood will listen to adult males singing around them. By the end of the summer, they will have learned the basic song of their species and often practise singing. However, males reared in second broods late in the summer, when the adult males have stopped singing, don't start to sing until the following spring. It's only then that they can learn the song. Young birds need to rehearse and their

incomplete songs are often referred to as sub-songs. While I'm speaking of Chaffinches, apparently research has shown that they also have distinctive accents: French Chaffinches sound different from Irish Chaffinches.

The sound quality of a bird's song can also be influenced by the habitats in which they reside. Birds of open country tend to produce crisp, sharp and loud notes, while the songs of woodland species tend to be softer (muffled) and quieter. This is because the dense vegetation of woodlands acts as an 'acoustic sponge', absorbing the sounds made by birds. The quality of the song may even reflect the quality of the territory a male has secured. Willow Warblers apparently sing slower if they have a poor territory, while those with better territories sing faster. It seems that females are more attracted to the faster singing males. This is also true for Swallows. Perhaps being able to sing faster may signal the health and strength of a male and the females are capable of picking up on these minute differences.

Many species combine song with flight displays. Meadow Pipits sing from a favourite perch before flying high into the air and circling the area while still in song. They then finish their song with a slow, open-winged 'parachute' glide back down to their favourite perch. Some birds use other methods to produce sounds. Snipe have stiff outer tail feathers that the bird spreads out during flight displays over his territory. Part of his display flight involves flying high into the sky and then dropping towards the ground in a steep dive. As he dives, his outer tail feathers vibrate when the air passes over them, creating a very distinctive humming or whirring sound. This is known as 'drumming'. Speaking of drumming … woodpeckers 'drum' on tree trunks to proclaim their territories and many will select trees that produce maximum sound transmission and resonance.

Other birds add to their song by borrowing phrases of songs from other species. Starlings bring this one step further by not only borrowing bird songs but also copying a whole assortment of other sounds. Their song is an extremely complex one, with bursts of notes mixed with bill clapping (sounding like rapid mini-castanets). Listening to Starlings can give you a clue as to where the birds may have been reared or lived. I've heard them do perfect imitations of Curlews, Oystercatchers and Redshanks, as well as the best Corncrake call I've ever heard (even better than the local Corncrakes themselves). I have even heard Starlings do 'wolf whistles' (building-site birds) and car alarms (obviously birds from rough neighbourhoods). Indeed, some have recently starting impersonating mobile phones. Apparently, in London during World War II, Starlings caused all sorts of problems when they started mimicking the sounds of dropping bombs. Why would a bird imitate other sounds? Is there a benefit to mimicry? The general thinking is that it takes a long time for a bird to learn so many sounds. The broader a bird's repertoire, the longer the bird has lived. If a bird has an impressive repertoire, then he is obviously an experienced individual … and therefore irresistibly attractive to females.

Song is what we traditionally consider to be the 'language of birds', but they also communicate in many other ways. This can start before the chick even emerges from the egg. Many parent birds begin to communicate with their chicks, and the chicks with their parents, before they hatch. This imprints the sound on both chick and parent and creates a bond between the two, allowing them to recognise each other by call. In other species, chicks actually

Starlings are great mimics — the more varied the song, the more impressive it is to females *(Clive Timmons)*

communicate with one another before they hatch. It is thought that this may allow some to synchronise their hatching.

Of course, as soon as a chick is hatched, the first thing it has to do is beg for food. For those birds that stay in the nest until they are old enough to fly, they get food by giving high-pitched begging calls and opening their beaks wide to expose their bright gapes (the inside of the beak). For those that leave the nest very quickly after hatching, they get fed mostly by giving begging calls (it isn't wise to expose that bright gape if you want to remain inconspicuous). Besides

the begging call, the chicks can give a call of distress that will immediately attract the parents. Likewise, the parents give several calls that the chicks understand instantly, including contact calls that often serve to bring the chicks together under the protective wing of a parent and alarm calls that may be a signal to hide or to stay still.

In fact, alarm calls are one of the most frequently heard bird vocalisations. Take a stroll through a woodland and you may be aware that there is a rolling sound of calls moving just ahead of you. These calls are alerting all birds to your presence. Alarm calls are

This Mallard chick can make and understand a variety of sounds — begging calls, contact calls and alarm calls
(*Annette Cutts*)

Long-tailed Tits call to each other frequently, enabling the family group to stay together in thick undergrowth *(John Finn)*

usually far-carrying, loud calls and many species' calls sound very alike. For example, the 'tik' alarm calls of a Robin are very like those of Wrens and Blackcaps. Alarm calls can also have an urgency to them. The rattling calls of Mistle Thrushes and the panicky 'chup-chup' calls (often accompanied by wing flutters) of Blackbirds are enough to cause an instant reaction among other birds. This makes perfect sense, given the fact that something that poses a threat to one species of bird, like a bird of prey or a fox, also poses a threat to others. So, most birds understand that they need to be on full alert when they hear the alarm calls of other birds, and then add their own calls to alert yet more to the potential danger. Birds will also come together to 'mob' a predator, such as a falcon or an owl. Surrounding their enemy and calling loudly exposes the owl or falcon; if the birds all band together, this is often enough to force the predator out of the area.

Birds that flock together also keep in touch by using calls. Contact calls are essential for night-flying migrants, like Redwings. On cool, still nights from early winter onwards, the high-pitched 'tseep' calls of these winter thrushes flying in loose flocks overhead are a common sound. The birds can't see each other, so the flock stays together by calling constantly. Waders also employ the same tactics when migrating. Most flocking species are very vocal, with geese and ducks always 'talking' to each other when flying. Warblers, like Chiffchaffs, are constantly calling to each other when feeding at migration stopovers. Even in woodlands, the short, low calls of Long-tailed Tits help to keep the flock in the same area while they are feeding. This is especially important as they may lose sight of each other as they move from place to place.

The vocalisations of birds are complex and highly evolved. Calls keep flocks together, stimulate parents to feed chicks and communicate messages of danger. Songs establish who the birds are, where they are and what they want (a mate). I know birds sing for very specific scientific reasons, but can you imagine spring without birdsong? How quiet the world would seem without the language of birds.

Chapter 7

Summer Birdwatching

Golden Plover *(Anthony McGeehan)*

'Summertime and the living is easy' … those opening words from that famous song might well have been written by a birdwatcher. Summer is indeed a time for taking it easy. In fact, many birdwatchers view summer as the time to chill out. It's a time to recover from the mayhem of the spring migration and to prepare mentally and emotionally for the autumn ahead. It's a very brief resting period between one

A visit to a Gannet colony in summer is an unforgettable experience *(Adrian Dancy)*

hectic birdwatching season and the next. Enjoy it while you can, however, because for the birdwatcher, summer only lasts from the beginning of June to the end of July (sometimes earlier, depending on when the first of the returning migrants are seen). It may be a time for easy living … but it's a very short time.

Come June, it seems that everything in the world of birds has settled down. Migrant birds that were planning to breed in Ireland have now arrived and are nesting and rearing young. Most of our resident birds are also very busy with the pressures of the breeding season, although for some that season might be over already. There is still a dawn chorus in June, but by July, it is but a brief burst of song. Birds are either too busy feeding young or have finished breeding. Have you ever noticed how hard it is to find a Robin in July? The reason is that once they have finished breeding, most birds undergo their post-nuptial moult. Moulting flight feathers means a bird may not be as quick to fly as earlier in the season, so it's better to be as inconspicuous as they can. Birds like Robins seem to fade away during July.

Having said all that, summer is a wonderful time to go birdwatching. The weather can be lovely and with those long evenings, it can be an ideal time to visit many habitats. One of the best summer birdwatching experiences is to take in the sights, sounds and smells of a seabird colony. Activity at these colonies is usually in full swing by June. There

Rathlin Island, Co. Antrim — home to the largest Guillemot colony in Ireland *(Anthony McGeehan)*

Razorbill *(Adrian Dancy)*

Guillemot and chick *(Adrian Dancy)*

Kittiwakes *(Michael Finn)*

A busy tern colony *(Anthony McGeehan)*

is a constant arrival and departure of adult birds from the colony as ever-hungry chicks are fed. There is also the constant sound of bickering adults crammed, high-rise fashion, onto steep cliff ledges. As an island nation, we are lucky to have so many wonderful colonies to visit. In fact, our seabird colonies are among the largest in Europe and we are the envy of many of our European neighbours.

Some of the best colonies can be viewed easily from land. Among these are Howth Head in Dublin, Bray and Wicklow Heads in Wicklow, the Old Head of Kinsale in Cork and the famous Cliffs of Moher in Clare. Of course, there are many smaller colonies on other headlands, and many seabirds can be seen extremely well in places like Dunmore East and Brownstown Head in Waterford. An even more

rewarding and enjoyable aspect to summer birdwatching is to visit one of the offshore islands. Rathlin Island in Antrim, Ireland's Eye in Dublin and the Great Saltee Island in Wexford are among the key summer places to visit, while in Kerry the dramatic Skellig Islands are home to over 28,000 pairs of Gannets as well as the largest breeding numbers of Storm Petrels in the world. Gannets will remain at the breeding colonies well into September, but many seabirds will have left the cliffs by July. Razorbill and Guillemot chicks behave in an almost suicidal way when they are barely a week old: they leap from the cliffs and glide (or fall slowly) down to their parents, who wait on the water below. They then swim out to sea where they will remain with their parents until they are old enough to fend for themselves. By mid-summer, they will be well away from the breeding colonies, but many other seabirds will still be attending young on the cliffs and islands well into late July.

In summer, many of these islands have regular ferry services, but always be careful when visiting seabird colonies. By their very nature, they are among the most dangerous places to visit. Cliff edges can be soft and give way easily, while unseen rabbit burrows can trip the unwary.

Another noisy summer experience are the tern colonies. Like the seabirds, by June these are a hive of activity. We have some wonderful tern colonies in Ireland. On the east coast, there is the small island of Rockabill, off Skerries, in Dublin. This is home to the rare Roseate Tern as well as Common, Arctic and Sandwich Terns. These birds can easily be watched feeding offshore. Another excellent location for watching terns is Dublin Port — it's not unusual to have Arctic and Common Terns feeding along the River Liffey as far upriver as the city centre. How many other capital cities in Europe can boast terns feeding in their city centres? A walk along the South Wall (Poolbeg) any evening will provide excellent views of these birds. Further south, the small islands off Dalkey are also excellent for seeing terns, and it seems that Roseate Terns are now establishing a colony there.

Rockabill Island, off the coast of Dublin, holds one of the most important tern colonies in Ireland *(Terry Flanagan)*

Common Tern *(Terry Flanagan)*   Roseate Tern *(Terry Flanagan)*   Arctic Tern *(Anthony McGeehan)*

In Wicklow, a stroll along the shingle beach at Kilcoole in summer will afford excellent views of Ireland's smallest tern, the Little Tern. BirdWatch Ireland has tern wardens in place every summer and they will show you the birds and explain the work that is being done to protect them.

Lying in the sunny south-east of the country, Wexford is a regular summer destination for many people. It is also home to a wealth of breeding birds, including the superb tern colonies of Lady's Island Lake. Here you can easily see Sandwich, Arctic and Common Terns as well as the exquisite Roseate Tern.

Lady's Island and Tacumshin Lakes in Wexford, and Kilcoole and Broad Lough in Wicklow, are among the best wetlands to visit in summer. As well as having reedbeds that attract warblers like Sedge, Grasshopper and Reed Warblers, they also have good open stretches of water where both Great Crested and Little Grebes, resplendent in their summer plumages, are easily seen. Water Rails are present in such wetlands, although they are very elusive — their pig-like squeals are often the only indication that they are there.

It's not just the coastal areas that attract nesting terns and gulls. Many of the inland lakes have such colonies, and areas like Lough Derg in Tipperary (to name but one) are always worth visiting. Like the Wexford wetlands, the reedbeds and open water attract a whole range of breeding warblers, grebes and ducks.

One of the rarest breeding terns in Ireland is the Little Tern *(Michael Finn)*

In June, our woodlands are alive with many species. With the dense canopy cover, it really is an 'eyes and ears' birdwatching experience. Unfortunately, we don't have many large areas of mature deciduous woodlands (hence we don't have large numbers of species like Redstarts and Wood Warblers). Some of the best woodlands can be found in Glendalough in Wicklow and Killarney in Kerry. In summer, migrants that are found in most deciduous woodlands include the highly vocal warblers like Chiffchaff and Willow Warbler, which sing high in the canopy. In recent years, Blackcaps have become more numerous and will certainly be heard (although rarely seen) in summer. Resident species will also be very active and June is a good time to possibly encounter the shy Jay as well as Treecreepers and Long-tailed Tits.

The mountains are also home to many other species. The upland bogs of the Wicklow Mountains and the Slieve Blooms (Offaly) are among the best for finding Red Grouse. In early summer, the adult males can be very vocal, giving their distinctive 'go-back' calls. They are hard to see and it may take a lot of walking to find them, but they are worth the effort. Skylarks and Meadow Pipits are also very common on the upland bogs in summer, while on some of the upland lakes and fast upland rivers of Wicklow, Goosanders can often be found. These birds are recent colonists and make a beautiful addition to a summer day's birdwatching.

Sadly, the evocative song and call of the Ring Ouzel is no longer a common summer sound on our mountainous scree slopes. Once found in most high mountain ranges, these birds are becoming increasingly scarce. On the positive side, however, Peregrine Falcons seem to be doing very well and breeding Wheatears are still found in these high, rocky areas. The normally elusive Dipper, a white-water

A summer woodland *(Joe Curtis)*

Peregrine Falcons, once threatened with extinction in Ireland, are now common *(Anthony McGeehan)*

river specialist, is also a bird more easily seen in summer when it becomes less shy (too busy finding food for begging chicks).

Another evocative but rare sound of the summer is that of the Corncrake. Once a widespread species found in every county, the Corncrake is now a globally endangered species with an increasingly fragmented population. Its rasping 'crek-crek' call, once a familiar sound of the Irish countryside, is now little more than a memory in many of its former breeding areas. While parts of Eastern Europe contain small breeding populations, the Shannon Callows of Offaly and Tory Island in Donegal represent some of the last strongholds in Western Europe. Corncrakes are rare and elusive birds that call from dense hay meadows (their favoured habitat). In summer, you're lucky if you catch a glimpse of one moving through the grass or calling, head up, looking for trespassing males. It's important that no disturbance is caused to

these birds, so patience is a virtue. By June, the grass is usually so high that seeing one is virtually impossible. However, a still summer's night is the best time for hearing them, when their calls carry over long distances in the cool night air. Many people holiday on the River Shannon in summer and anyone who visits Banagher in Co. Offaly should take a stroll along the nearby meadows or listen for the birds from the bridge in the town. The calling of a Corncrake is a rare privilege to hear in Ireland in the 21st century.

Last, but by no means least, are our towns, parks and hedgerows. Ireland's hedgerows are a unique feature of our countryside. The thousands of kilometres of hedgerows that meander across the landscape are home to resident birds like Wrens, Robins, Dunnocks and Blackbirds. In summer, these ancient land boundaries are alive with the songs of visiting warblers like Whitethroats and Chiffchaffs. Our gardens and parks are like mini-woodlands in a

Corncrakes are now restricted to just a few sites in Ireland
(Anthony McGeehan)

Willow Warblers are one of our commonest summer visitors
(Michael Finn)

cement wilderness, providing rich food and safe nesting sites. In our cities, a recent feature of summer is the nocturnal singing of Blackbirds and Robins. This is caused by what is known as a 'false dawn', when the impression of the first rays of daylight is created by streetlights. As these birds are usually the first to sing at dawn, it is these two species that are most affected.

This Sooty Tern was one of the avian surprises of 2005, here being harrassed by an Arctic Tern *(Gearóid O'Sullivan)*

As the summer season ends, the first waders begin to return to the estuaries from their breeding grounds. Many of these are adults that have failed to breed successfully and are moving south earlier than most other waders. Of course, it isn't just failed breeding waders that can occur in late summer — any migrant bird that has failed to breed during the early summer months may start 'drifting'. It's not unusual to find European warblers, for example, at this time of year. Like the waders, these tend to be adults that are slightly off course and many can often still be in 'breeding mode'. I remember seeing (and hearing) a superb Savi's Warbler in full song at Tacumshin Lake in Wexford in the third week of July. He stayed for almost a week and sang constantly … sadly, in vain.

Terns are another group of birds that tend to drift if they have not bred successfully. Many rare terns are found in July and, like the waders at this time of year, they are usually adult birds. European species like White-winged Black Terns can occasionally be found with roosting terns along all coastlines, while the larger and rarer Gull-billed Tern prefers more freshwater wetlands. Areas such as Tacumshin Lake in Wexford and Ballycotton in Cork seem to be magnets for these species as they not only have suitable habitats but also attract large numbers of terns. So it's always worth checking the flocks of terns along the coast from mid-July onwards. Take it from me … it really is worth doing. In July 2005, a Sooty Tern was found with the tern colony at Rockabill in Dublin. The closest this bird breeds to Ireland is in the South Atlantic. One of my best Irish birdwatching moments came in the same month when I was out looking for the Sooty Tern. On a beach in Meath, I discovered an Elegant Tern with Sandwich Terns. This carrot-orange-billed tern belongs on the Pacific coast of North America and was the last thing I expected to see.

Summer can indeed be a time for taking it easy. Autumn may be just around the corner, but relax and enjoy the summer months. Take it easy, but always be prepared for the unexpected … summertime can throw many surprises your way.

Chapter 8

The Nesting Season

Ringed Plover *(Warren Hewitt)*

As March slips gently into April, it's great to know that spring has at last arrived. Around us, our resident birds are busy proclaiming their territories and selecting suitable nest sites. Already the first of our summer visitors are reaching our shores, and shortly they too will be nest-building. But what are nests? Put

Ringed Plover nest *(Sean Cronin)*

simply, nests are where birds lay their eggs, incubate those eggs and, for many species, where the chicks remain until they are fledged (ready to leave the nest).

Most people, if asked what a nest was, would describe a cup-shaped object made of grasses wedged in between branches in a tree. Such a description would be right … many birds do build nests exactly like that. However, just as there are many species of birds, there is also a vast array of nest designs and nesting places. In fact, there are some birds that don't bother to build nests at all. It's also important to remember that nests are a purely summer residence for birds — once the breeding season is over, they are no longer required and are abandoned. Nests vary from simple hollows scraped in the ground, like those of Ringed Plovers, to highly elaborate and beautiful constructions, like those of Long-tailed Tits.

Many birds choose to nest on the ground and these employ many different strategies for nesting. Some birds, like Guillemots and Razorbills, simply lay their eggs on the ledges of the steepest cliffs. There is no attempt to even construct a nest. The eggs are cone-shaped, so if a parent bird should knock against it when leaving the ledge, the egg will simply roll in a tight circle; if it were more rounded, it might roll off the edge. Other seabirds, like Gannets, nest on similar steep cliffs but build a large, cup-shaped nest of seaweed and other coastal material, including discarded fishing netting. These birds rely on the fact

Lapwing with chick *(Anthony McGeehan)*

Gannet with chick *(Adrian Dancy)*

that their nests are located on such steep cliffs, which means potential predators simply cannot reach them. Many ground-nesting seabirds also choose islands that are predator-free. Birds of prey, like Kestrels and Peregrine Falcons, very often nest on ledges of cliffs too and also, in some cities, on the ledges of high-rise buildings; they will even use old, abandoned Raven nests.

Other birds that nest on the ground tend to rely on camouflage to protect their nest location. Many ground-nesting birds, such as Ringed Plovers, Lapwings and Skylarks, sit tight on the nest and simply blend into their surroundings. When they leave the nest, their eggs and chicks are also perfectly camouflaged. Gulls and terns also rely on the camouflage of their patterned eggs and chicks to make them almost impossible for predators to see. Swans also nest on the ground and build large nests of weed and feathers. Like all wildfowl (ducks, geese and swans), the chicks are hatched with down feathers (most chicks have no feathers at all when they hatch). Within a day, the nest is abandoned and all the chicks take to the water with their parents.

Many species prefer to nest off the ground, in the relative safety of bushes or trees. At least here, ground predators are unable to reach the eggs or chicks … although there are always others eager to rob the eggs and take the chicks as well. Many of these birds build more complicated nests than the ground-nesters, with cup-shaped nests made of grasses, straw and even dung. Species like the Blackbird will also use mud to strengthen the construction. Once the main frame of the nest is complete, the birds line the nest with feathers, animal hair and grasses. At the point where the nest is almost complete, the female (which in many cases does most of the incubation) will frequently sit deep into the nest and move her body from side to side to ensure that the inner nest is

A Lapwing nest — a slight indentation in the ground *(Anthony McGeehan)*

The floating nest of a Moorhen *(Adrian Dancy)*

comfortable and fits perfectly to her body size. When sitting on the eggs, she needs to make sure that they are not exposed to any cold air. Cup-shaped nests make perfect sense: they are usually deep enough for the parent to sit and incubate the eggs comfortably, and when the chicks emerge, are too deep for them to fall out. If a tree-nesting chick falls from the nest, it is usually doomed as there is no way for it to climb back in.

Another cup-shaped-nest builder is the Swallow. They build a nest made of tiny mud pellets that dry out and form the main frame of the nest. The nest is then lined with feathers and hair before the female lays the eggs. These nests can sometimes be so well built that they are used year after year, with the returning birds having to do no more than a little bit of repair work each spring. The smallest bird in Ireland, the Goldcrest, builds the smallest nest. It is made of lichen and moss and lined with feathers and hair. Some tree-nesting birds go one better and build a nest with a roof. The most elaborate nest is that of the Long-tailed Tit. They construct a domed, rugby ball-shaped nest of lichens, spiders' webs and feathers, with an entrance hole at the side. Inside the nest, the incubating adult, the eggs and, when they hatch, the chicks, are warm and snug, tucked away from the elements. In many ways, Long-tailed Tits could almost be described as hole-nesters.

Swallows' nests are very strong and can last for years, but it can be a snug fit for growing chicks *(Joe Curtis)*

Hole-nesters, as the name suggests, are birds that choose to build a nest totally under cover. This can be simply a hole in a wall or tree or, as in many gardens, in specially erected nest-boxes. Nesting in a hole offers great advantages: it can be difficult for a predator to attack the nest eggs or chicks; the nest can't be seen; and, finally, the adult bird and the eggs/chicks are protected from the weather outside. One of the commonest hole-nesters is the Blue Tit. These birds readily take to nest-boxes. The male will select the nest site and, once the female gives her approval, both set about creating a nest of grasses and straw. This forms the base of the nest and the female, like the cup-nesters, will create a cup shape that fits snugly around her for the incubation period. The nest is then lined with feathers and hair; groomed pet hair is a favourite lining. It's ironic to think of young Blue Tits snuggling in against a big ball of cat hair, isn't it?

Another hole-nesting bird is the Starling. They will use holes in walls, trees or even go into holes in roofs of houses. Other birds excavate their own nest holes. Sand Martins (close cousins of the Swallow) dig out a long entrance tunnel that leads to a nesting chamber. These are usually found on steep sand dunes and on the faces of quarries. Some have even been known to use the faces of cut-away bogs. Another bird that excavates a nest hole is the Kingfisher. They nest on the banks of rivers and at some locations will even

Long-tailed Tits build very elaborate nests *(Joe Curtis)*

use specially constructed 'Kingfisher walls' overlooking a river. These 'walls' have nesting tunnels already built into them.

Finally, I can't leave the subject of nests and nest-building without mentioning one very special species — the Cuckoo. Cuckoos have evolved a unique approach to rearing their young. They do not build any nest at all. In fact, they don't have anything to do with raising their families. They lay their eggs in the nests of other species. The eggs are usually the same colour and pattern as those of the host species. So as not to raise suspicion, when the female Cuckoo lays an egg, she removes one of the other eggs from the nest. This way, when the host bird returns, she won't think that there are too many eggs in the nest. Once the Cuckoo chick (which, by the way, resembles a weightlifter on steroids) is hatched, it will push all the other eggs and chicks out of the nest and receive the undivided attention of the poor host birds that spend their summer feeding this enormous and ever-hungry chick. With no chicks to look after, the adult Cuckoos usually leave Ireland by August and head south at their leisure. The young Cuckoos depart in September, leaving behind very exhausted foster parents.

Whatever the nest design and strategy of nesting, you can be sure that each one is designed to offer the best protection and safety for the eggs. Of course, without the eggs there will be no chicks. Put simply, an egg is like a cocoon that provides everything a growing chick needs (except heat). The yoke provides a rich store of food while the sticky substance we know as the 'white of the egg' (correctly known as the albumen) not only cushions the yoke but also provides water, insulation and additional food that will eventually be consumed by the chick.

The formation of eggs is similar to a complex factory production line. As egg production can be quite physically demanding for the female, only one egg is produced at a time, and to produce this egg, the female needs to be fit and well-fed. As an ovum is released from the ovary, it becomes attached to the yoke. The egg and yoke then drop into the abdomen before continuing down the oviduct. In the oviduct, stored sperm (often held in small 'storage sacks' for days or even weeks) will fertilise the egg. The fact that the female can store sperm has a very important impact for males that assist with rearing young. In order to ensure that they are indeed the fathers of their

Arctic Tern chick — waiting to be fed can be very tiring at times! *(Anthony McGeehan)*

young, males stay close by the females after mating. Females can often copulate with more than one male (when her mate isn't there) and the last thing the male wants is to exert all of his energy and time raising another male's offspring. Male Dunnocks, for example, don't trust their females at all, and before copulation takes place, will peck at the female's cloaca (vent), resulting in any stored sperm being ejected. Then, and only then, can he be really sure that he has fertilised the eggs that are laid.

The next stage is that the fertilised egg is covered by the albumen before a thin membrane and the shell (secreted by a lime-producing gland) are laid over the complete package. Pigment is added to the eggshell at this stage to give it colour, while specks of blood and bile create the speckles and blotches on the egg at the very final section of the production line. In some species, the egg twists in the oviduct at this stage and this creates a pattern of lines and squiggles instead of speckles and blotches. The egg is then ready to be laid. Most birds that nest in holes produce white or pale eggs. There is no need for their eggs to be camouflaged. Eggs provide a very rich source of food for many predators, so birds that nest in the open, like Lapwings, produce darker eggs with heavy speckling and blotches because camouflage is an issue for them.

Interestingly, cell division commences during this production-line process, with a tiny embryo forming inside the egg before it is laid. Heat is what triggers cell division, and the heat inside the female's body is enough to start the process. However, once the egg is laid, the development of the embryo stops and will not commence again until incubation begins. It's as if the embryo has gone into a mini-state of suspended animation or hibernation. At this stage, the tiny embryo does not need heat to survive.

The production of an egg from start to finish can take up to two days in large birds, but only one day in smaller species. Once the incubation process begins, the embryos emerge from their 'suspended animation' and begin developing again. The eggshell is fragile and porous. Inside, the chick needs to be able to breathe in oxygen from the outside world and release carbon dioxide. When it comes to hatching, the eggshell must be thin enough to allow the chick to break through. The process of egg production is the same for all species, but once laid, many birds adopt different tactics for incubating the eggs. Some start incubating as soon as each egg is laid; others wait until the entire clutch of eggs is laid before starting.

Most small birds adopt the latter strategy. Waiting until all the eggs are laid before beginning to incubate them means that the eggs will hatch more or less at the same time. This is called synchronous hatching and is usually timed to coincide with an abundance of food. This works well most seasons, but it means that should there be a food shortage, most (and sometimes all) of the chicks may die.

Many larger birds and most birds of prey choose a different method, preferring to commence the incubation of an egg as soon as it's laid. In these cases, the first egg laid will hatch first, the second egg laid will hatch second, and so on. As it can take two days for large birds to produce each egg, this means that there will be an age gap of at least two days between each chick. If four eggs hatch, the first chick can be more than a week older than the last chick. This method is called asynchronous hatching. So are there any advantages to having chicks of differing ages and

Common Tern eggs are uniquely patterned *(Michael O'Clery)*

sizes within the one nest? In times of a plentiful food supply, it doesn't really matter because all the chicks will be fed well. When there are food shortages, however, the oldest (and therefore the biggest) will be fed first. Sometimes the oldest chick becomes the bully and smaller chicks struggle to be fed at all. In many cases, the last chick hatched will die because it's usually too small to compete successfully for food. When this happens, the oldest chick may eat the body of his or her younger sibling. Such cannibalism makes perfect sense — it would be wasteful not to avail of such a valuable source of food when times are hard. In some years, all but the oldest chick survives. This may seem a cruel and unfair system, but it ensures that at least one chick fledges.

Struggling free from an egg is hard work for a chick. The inside of an egg is very confined and movement is restricted. A young chick simply does not have the room to move its head in order to break free by pecking at the inside of the shell. As well as this, the beak is still quite soft, but it is armed with a small, hard spike, usually towards the tip of the bill. This is called the 'egg-tooth', and by pressing hard against one spot inside the egg with this spike, the chick can crack the shell. It will then usually start kicking and pushing inside the egg until it eventually breaks free.

The nesting season is a very busy time for parent birds. As each egg hatches, the parents remove the shell from the nest because the white inside of a shell may draw attention to the nest site. The parents will also remove the droppings of their chicks from the nest, which is presented to them in a small faecal sac (the dropping is in a small membranous bag). This prevents the nest site from getting dirty, and a white trail of droppings would quickly attract potential predators. For birds that nest under cover (Swallows) or on the safety of steep cliffs (Kittiwakes), the young simply deposit their droppings over the side of the nest. Leaving a trail of droppings won't bring unwanted attention for them.

With chicks begging to be fed constantly, the adults are working flat out from dawn to dusk. People often wonder if they should leave food out for birds in summer, sometimes fearing that peanuts, for example, may be fed to young birds and they will choke when

The 'egg-tooth' of this Lesser Black-backed Gull is just visible, as the chick struggles to break the shell *(Michael O'Clery)*

trying to swallow them. This rarely happens. Adults know what to feed their young. Leaving food out means that adults have a quick and easy food source for themselves, thus allowing more time to find food for their young. I've also seen adult Blue Tits take a peanut and 'pare' it down to a small size suitable to be given to an older chick. Most small birds require an abundance of insects to feed their young, so think twice before spraying your roses to rid them of aphids and caterpillars … a nesting pair of tits or Robins will clear them for you.

The stimuli to feed the chicks are usually the begging calls and the bright gapes (mouths) of their young. All young birds tend to have bright yellow, orange or red gapes and many even have small spots which, when seen in ultraviolet, act like landing lights, ensuring the parents don't miss their targets. So strong is the urge to feed young, it's not unusual for a bird that is still in 'chick-feeding mode' to stop and feed the young of another bird species. They just can't resist those bright gapes! There are even wonderful images taken some years ago of House Sparrows feeding goldfish in a pond. When the fish came to the surface (as goldfish do), the sparrows saw their bright orange mouths and began feeding the fish. Realising that they were onto a good thing, the goldfish kept coming to the surface and the birds kept feeding them. This apparently went on for some time. I'm sure the adult sparrows were wondering to themselves whether these 'hungry chicks' would ever fledge.

There comes a time when the chicks will leave the nest. The timing of this depends entirely on the species involved. For many waterbirds, it happens within hours of hatching. Most small birds leave the nest after two or three weeks, while many larger birds can take up to two months or longer. Once they leave the nest, the young birds will usually disperse to different areas within their parents' territory. The reason why they disperse is because this is one of the most dangerous times for a young bird. They are usually weak at flying and can be caught easily by predators. If they all stayed together, all the young birds could be taken at once. It makes perfect sense for them to sit tight in different places. The parents can locate the chicks by their begging calls. Many people find young birds at this stage of their development and mistakenly consider them abandoned chicks. This is usually not the case. The parent will eventually come

Common Tern chicks — these are very young as each still has an egg-tooth on the tip of its bill *(Michael O'Clery)*

Juvenile Dipper — young birds have a lot to learn … like you can't eat a stick! *(Adrian Dancy)*

A young Wren, waiting for the next feed *(John Fox)*

A hungry young House Sparrow, begging for food from its mother *(John Fox)*

back and feed it in turn. The worst thing to do is to bring it home with you and try to raise it yourself. If it's in the open, bring it into an area of cover close by. Only if it is in extreme danger should you remove it from where you have found it. If that danger passes, put it back where you found it as quickly as possible.

For many species, once all of the chicks are fully independent, they will begin the whole process again. Some species will attempt to have two or three broods in a season. Swallows have raised four broods successfully in recent summers, taking advantage of the warmer autumnal days to raise young into September and even October. Others, like Blue Tits, invest all their energies into raising just one large brood. When that brood has been fledged successfully, the Blue Tits have done their duty for another year.

Once fledged, young birds are relying on what they have learned to survive. Some are only six weeks old or less when they face the world alone. They must be able to fend for themselves, find enough food to survive, be aware of dangers, and be strong enough to escape when danger threatens. For those that migrate, they may need to build up enough fat reserves for long flights ahead, and for many migrant birds, they face the dangers of those long migrations without the

assistance of adults. They need to find the way by themselves. For non-migratory birds, they are facing a winter when food may be scarce and weather may be severe. It's no wonder that the mortality rate for many young birds is so high. It's estimated, for example, that 70 per cent of all young Swallows that leave Ireland each autumn will die in their first year. All young birds face many tough challenges in their first months on this Earth. Only the strongest survive. That any survive at all is remarkable.

When the breeding season ends, the nest sites fall silent and empty. The process of finding and defending territories, building nests and raising young is a major investment for all adult birds. It's also essential for the future of their species. For many small birds, they may only have one breeding season in their short lives. This may be their only chance to pass on their genes. Birds are under so many pressures these days, ranging from habitat loss to climate change, that they really do need as many young birds as possible to fledge each year just to keep their populations stable. Each summer, I hope that our birds have a successful breeding season ahead. The chicks of today are the breeding adults of tomorrow.

Chapter 9

Autumn Birdwatching

Wryneck *(Eric Dempsey)*

As with the official first day of spring, there seems to be some confusion as to when exactly autumn begins. Like springtime, it all depends on what the season actually means to you. Many people I know head off on 'summer' holidays in August ... so August is still the summer for them. Others view the first day of September as officially the beginning of autumn.

Headlands and islands, like Great Saltee in Wexford, are the first landfall for many migrants *(Clive Timmons)*

Many argue that autumn hasn't arrived until the leaves on the trees turn golden brown. If that were the case, then autumn might not be starting until November given the trend of recent years ... an old Oak tree near where I live doesn't begin to shed its leaves until December.

For the birdwatcher, however, the seasons are easy to define. Spring is when the first spring migrants arrive, and autumn begins when the autumn migration gets under way. That usually happens in earnest by the second week of August, but can start off as early as the beginning of the month. Autumn ends when that migration ends, which is usually at the end of October, although in some years the season can stretch to the second week of November. So in any given year, the birdwatcher can view autumn as lasting from the beginning of August to mid-November. Autumn is a great changing of the guard. The winter birds are taking over the country from the summer visitors, while others are simply passing through. For the resident birds, it's time to prepare for the winter ahead.

Autumn birdwatching is perhaps one of the most exciting and unpredictable times of the year. There are many differences between spring and autumn migration. The obvious one is the general direction in which the birds are travelling. In spring, it is roughly a south–north movement; in autumn, it's generally a north–south one. Another big difference is the sheer number of birds on the move. The autumn migration involves all the adult migrant birds that have survived the summer and all of their surviving offspring. Birds like Swallows, for example, are capable of rearing as many as 15–20 young each summer. So while just two adults birds arrived in spring, as many as 22 birds (the two adults and 20 young) could be flying south in autumn. Given that birds such as Swallows suffer a mortality rate of 70 per cent in their first year, the number of birds returning each spring is always significantly less. The third difference is that, as so many of the migrating birds are immature birds making the journey for the first time, the possibility of them getting lost is higher than in spring, when returning birds have at least one migration 'under their belt'. Finally, the other major factor is weather. In autumn, migrating birds face far more unpredictable and extreme weather systems than they might in spring. The other thing worth remembering is that identifying birds in autumn can be a little more difficult. Many are in immature plumages and very few adults appear as bright or smart-looking as they are in spring.

Autumn usually kicks off with the first trickle of returning waders. Early August is a superb time to begin watching the tidal estuaries and mudflats for wader flocks. The commonest wader we see at this time of the year is the Dunlin, a small bird with a

A juvenile Red-backed Shrike *(Warren Hewitt)*

down-curved bill. While we have small numbers of breeding Dunlin, the first birds that appear on our shorelines in early August are usually adult birds that have had an unsuccessful breeding season in more northerly areas, like Scandinavia and Iceland. There really is no point in these birds remaining on the breeding grounds, so they move south ahead of the main flocks. As there is safety in numbers, and as most waders tend to travel in flocks, these early returning Dunlin flocks often contain other waders that have also failed to breed. Many of these may even be North American species that crossed the Atlantic in previous autumns and have been travelling on the 'wrong side' since then. Other birds that can occur this early in the season may be Siberian species, such as Red-necked Stint, which may be thousands of kilometres off course. Occasionally, other European waders, like Little Stints and Curlew Sandpipers, join these flocks. At this time of year, all of these birds are usually in full adult summer plumage (or in the early process of moulting). Any tidal estuary or coastal wetland that attracts Dunlin flocks in August can conceivably hold other waders.

As August fades into September, the numbers of returning waders increase and by then you'll find that there are now many young birds (juveniles) within the flocks. Just like failed breeders, other juvenile waders will often join the flocks. This is therefore the best

Dunlin, *the* common wader of autumn *(Anthony McGeehan)*

time to look for Little Stints and Curlew Sandpipers with the Dunlin, while around reed-fringed coastal wetlands, more solitary Ruffs and Wood Sandpipers can occur. Depending on the weather systems and whether it has been a successful breeding season for these birds, numbers can vary from 'just a few' to hundreds. Some of the best wader hotspots from early August to September are the estuaries and mudflats along the eastern coast, from Antrim down into Wexford. Along the south coast, many birds tend to stop and feed before moving south (and out to sea). For that reason, areas in Wexford such as Tacumshin Lake and Lady's Island Lake can hold thousands of birds. Other famous wader-watching areas are found — for the same reasons — in Cork, with the likes of Ballycotton and the many tidal estuaries of West Cork worth visiting.

Every autumn at these locations, wader-watchers find an array of rare birds. September is the peak time for finding North American waders. Unlike those seen in early August, the majority of these are juveniles that have been blown into Europe. Like the adults, they too will be attracted to the Dunlin flocks. Occasionally some find each other, and at Tacumshin Lake it's not unusual to come across a 'mini-flock' of Buff-breasted Sandpipers. By mid-October, the main movement of waders has subsided. Those that are in Ireland are most likely here to stay. The rarer North American birds (with the occasional exception) usually move south for the winter (as they would if they were on the other side of the Atlantic).

August also sees the first southward movements of seabirds off our coasts. Most of our European breeding seabirds winter in the Atlantic and migrate south many kilometres out to sea. However, in certain weather conditions, these birds get blown closer to shore and can be seen from headlands and islands. The peak seabird migration time is from mid-August to

A Buff-breasted Sandpiper, a much sought-after rarity from North America. This bird was photographed in Wexford
(Eric Dempsey)

The Bridges of Ross in Clare. One of the best vantage points in Europe for observing seabird migration *(Victor Caschera)*

Manx Shearwaters breed around our coasts, but winter in waters off Brazil *(Anthony McGeehan)*

Sooty Shearwaters pass through Irish waters on their way to the South Atlantic *(Anthony McGeehan)*

Fastnet Rock, off Cape Clear Island in Cork *(Joe Curtis)*

late September. When winds are blowing in a north-westerly direction, areas like Kilcummin Head and Annagh Head in Mayo, the Bridges of Ross in Clare, Ramore Head in Antrim and Brandon Point in Kerry are the places to be. Birds flying south get blown close to our coastline and are forced to fly by these headlands in order to continue their journeys out into the Atlantic. Likewise, in Cork, headlands like Mizen Head, Galley Head and the Old Head of Kinsale, as well as Cape Clear Island, can witness spectacularly large movements of seabirds in south-westerly winds. Judging wind directions accurately is essential for seawatching. There is nothing worse than driving to Kilcummin Head expecting north-westerly winds and finding an easterly gale blowing when you get there. You'll spend your entire day staring at an empty sea.

By the end of September and the beginning of October, the main seabird migration has waned, which is just as well as this allows us to concentrate on other things. For many birdwatchers, this is 'the' time of the autumn because this is when the main migration of passerines takes place. Passerines are perching birds and include species like warblers, buntings, pipits and finches. From mid-September onwards, millions of

Great Shearwater *(Anthony McGeehan)*

birds are on the move all over Europe. Irish birds usually work their way south and depart from the most southern headlands and islands. At the same time, European birds are flying south through Europe, many crossing open areas of water, such as the Bay of Biscay. Should they hit strong head winds, the birds have little choice but to go with that wind. A head wind for a bird travelling south is a southerly or south-easterly wind (the direct opposite to the situation for the birds in spring). Therefore the same headlands and islands (with lighthouses) that are good in spring (Hook Head and Great Saltee Island in Wexford, Brownstown Head in Waterford, and the Old Head of Kinsale, Galley Head, Mizen Head and Cape Clear and Dursey Islands in Cork) are also excellent locations for watching for autumn migrants. Winds coming from a more northerly or westerly direction make headlands and islands along the north and west coasts better options for finding migrant birds. Hotspots along these coasts include Loop Head in Clare, Annagh Head in Mayo and Tory Island in Donegal.

During September and October, birdwatchers can be found at any (or sometimes all) of these locations, watching in the hope of finding that major rare bird. It takes dedication and hard work, but the rewards can be rich. Should we experience strong Atlantic gales, then the possibility of finding an American passerine is on everyone's mind. Seeing a forecast that predicts a strong Atlantic storm starts us salivating like Pavlov's dogs at the prospect of an American warbler feeding in a garden on an Irish headland. The headlands and islands that bear the brunt of the storm are most likely the places where that elusive American bird might be found.

As October slips into the darkness of November, the feeling of the end of the season descends upon us. While out birdwatching, there is a distinctly wintry feel to the birds we are seeing. Instead of autumn migrants, we're looking at geese, ducks and waders. Often there is a 'sting in the tail', however. In most years, November 'throws up' one last good bird and sometimes it's a major rarity. Often it's a Siberian species that has taken a long time to reach us. Sometimes it can be a late American species, blown

Lapland Bunting *(Michael O'Keeffe)*

across to Europe on a late Atlantic storm. It gives us all one last moment to savour before winter birdwatching takes over in earnest.

Besides the birds you might see in autumn, the great thing about the season is that, as birdwatchers, we visit a large variety of habitats as the season matures. Wader-watching turns to seabird-watching, which eventually turns to the hopeful and exciting prospects of rare passerines. Many birdwatchers live for the autumn months. No two autumns are ever the same. I suppose it's the uncertainty of this aspect of our pastime that makes it so wonderful. However, the one certainty about the autumn is that each year we, like the migrant birds, will once again find ourselves back at our favourite coastal habitats. Roll on the summer!

Chapter 10

Permission to Land? — Autumn Migration

Isabelline Shrike *(Sean Cronin)*

The morning of 24 November 1999 was dreadful. South-westerly winds were hitting Force 6 to Storm Force 8 and the heavy rain made driving very difficult. Yet here I was at 9.00am, standing along a narrow road above Ballyferriter village, near Dingle in Co. Kerry, having travelled down from Dublin throughout the early hours of the morning. Why, you may ask? Simple, really ... I was there to see a bird! This was not just any bird, however. No, this was a Brown Shrike — an avian superstar. Brown Shrikes breed in central Siberia, fly east to Japan and south into China. By late November, they are usually in their wintering areas, ranging from India to south-east Asia, Borneo and the Philippines. This was the first time a Brown Shrike had ever been seen in Ireland.

Every autumn, from late summer into early November, millions of birds are on the move. Ireland becomes an 'avian airport' of sorts. Departing on long-haul flights are birds like Swallows, journeying to far-off destinations like southern Africa, while Blackcaps are taking shorter flights to the Mediterranean Basin. In the arrivals lounge are geese, ducks and waders, migrating from northern Europe and the Arctic tundra, while the night flights carry

Brent Geese — migrants from Arctic Canada and Greenland *(Clive Timmons)*

Fieldfares and Redwings into the country. The transit lounge is also full, with many species simply stopping off in Ireland en route to other destinations. Most of these transit visitors are waders, like Little Stints and Curlew Sandpipers, although in recent years some of the latter have decided to winter here (a result of our milder winters, perhaps?).

Many of these flights have been planned well in advance, and the departure and arrival times are well understood by birdwatchers. At this stage, the migration routes of many species are known. Swallows winter in southern Africa, Brown Shrikes in India and south-east Asia. So why would a bird that should be wintering on the other side of the world turn up in Ireland instead?

One of the main reasons lies in understanding the important difference between spring and autumn migration. In spring, migrating birds are usually adults with migration experience. Some may have completed this journey many times over. In autumn, on the other hand, the majority of birds migrating are young and inexperienced and are making this journey for the first time. They are unfamiliar with the best routes and they simply get lost. This theory is supported by the fact that most 'rare birds' found each autumn in Ireland are invariably young birds. This seems the most likely and simple explanation. But can this really explain how, for example, an American warbler migrating from Canada to South America can suddenly turn up on an Irish headland in autumn? Or does it explain why a Siberian bird migrating to south-east Asia can turn up in Dingle? Are these birds simply lost, or are there other factors at play?

In the case of vagrant birds from North America, weather is perhaps one of the key factors. Lying on the western edge of Europe, Ireland is one of the first

Pectoral Sandpiper (Eric Dempsey)

Lesser Yellowlegs (Michael O'Keeffe)

landing points for transatlantic vagrants. In some years, it's not unusual to encounter five species of North American shorebird (Yankee waders) in one day, with the peak period stretching from early September into mid-October. In exceptional circumstances, small birds like warblers and thrushes can also reach our shores, but certainly not with the same regularity as waders.

The weather systems responsible for transporting such vagrants to this side of the Atlantic are now better understood. Many North American species migrate to South America down the western Atlantic coast, some undertaking non-stop flights. Leaving from sites in eastern Canada and north-east USA, it is believed that many leave in the wake of a cold front, taking advantage of the north-westerly tail wind. Problems occur when these migrants meet slower-moving depressions, requiring them to fly through the associated bad weather. Many birds, especially young birds, do not negotiate these weather systems successfully and are drifted out across the Atlantic on the westerly winds. Depending on the prevailing meteorological situation, these weather fronts can move very rapidly across the ocean, driven by the high-altitude jet streams. Birds caught out in these systems can either fight the wind or simply fly with it.

If the system is fast moving enough, it can reach the Irish coast within 48 hours and deposit its exhausted cargo of migrant birds. For that reason, many Irish birdwatchers watch the movements of hurricanes that track along the eastern US coast each autumn. These can develop into strong Atlantic depressions that race across the ocean and hit Ireland as severe storms. Many of the best North American birds I've seen in Ireland were usually in the aftermath of such storms.

White-rumped Sandpiper *(Sean Cronin)*

If the weather system takes any longer to move across, birds like warblers and thrushes will probably die in the middle of the ocean. I'm sure that for every one such bird that makes it to Ireland, many more are lost at sea. Waders, on the other hand, are much stronger, long-distance fliers. When they encounter weather systems that force them out into the Atlantic, they simply continue east, making landfall in Western Europe.

There may be other, more complicated factors at work, too. As most waders are high-altitude migrants, it may not be the low-level weather systems that bring birds across the Atlantic, but rather westerly airflows in the high-altitude jet stream. As a result, vagrants can occur despite the apparent lack of strong westerlies, arriving instead on jet streams that are undetectable on daily synoptic weather maps — the sort we consult when we want to check the likelihood of a vagrant being swept across the Atlantic. As some birds travel above the clouds, this may even account for the occurrence of species along the eastern and south-eastern coasts of Ireland and eastern Britain, with birds not dropping down until they see land.

There is one final consideration to take into account for the occurrence of North American birds. For birds to cross the Atlantic, regardless of the weather systems that may have brought them, they would still need to have enough stored fat reserves to

Golden Plovers are among the strongest of long-distance migrants (*Clive Timmons*)

make the journey in one flight. For example, North American warblers and thrushes only have enough stored fat reserves for journeys that last no more than three or four days. Recent research also shows that Greater Yellowlegs (a wader very like our Greenshank) may be capable of storing enough fat for a maximum journey of 2,650–2,850 km, compared to the maximum of 3,400 km for Lesser Yellowlegs (similar to Redshanks). Therefore it's only in exceptional circumstances that Greater Yellowlegs could reach Ireland, which may account for the rarity of that species here compared to Lesser Yellowlegs. It's worth noting, of course, that regardless of how they get here, the majority of North American birds found each autumn are young birds making the long migration for the first time.

While weather may account for the occurrence of species from North America, it can't really offer a useful explanation for birds that occur from the east ('Sibes', as birdwatchers fondly call them). Surely a bird beginning its migration from breeding areas in central or northern Siberia can't be blown off course by bad weather and end up in Western Europe? The distances these birds travel to get here are so great that any weather system that may have influenced them initially would have subsided long before they reached even Eastern Europe. And yet, they still turn up.

Booted Warblers usually winter in Asia. This one was photographed in Cork *(Michael O'Keeffe)*

A Red-throated Pipit, photographed in Dublin, but which should have been in Africa *(Derek Charles)*

As all migratory birds are born with a mini-compass enabling them to fly in the right direction, how can these birds get lost to such an extent that they end up in Ireland? One theory suggests that many of these birds originate from areas where there are magnetic anomalies, which could influence the accuracy of a bird's compass. This may account for some birds apparently migrating in the wrong direction.

Another theory is that of 'reverse migration'. It suggests that birds from the east actually fly to Ireland deliberately. If the theory of reverse migration is correct, it suggests that some birds are born with a slight defect that causes them to fly in the opposite direction to their normal routes. In other words, instead of flying south-east in the autumn, they will fly north-west.

To understand how this can affect migrant birds, it's important to remember that the world is a globe. Therefore if a bird is beginning its first migration from western or central Siberia in late summer, it should start flying south-east towards its wintering grounds in China. If, however, it starts heading north-west instead, where might it end up? Using a globe, the answer is simple — it will probably cross over the Ural Mountains, move through the Baltic and, by late autumn, may end up in Western Europe.

Of course, weather patterns can alter their direction when they reach the Baltic region or when they begin crossing the North Sea. As a result, strong north-easterly gales in late autumn usually result in the occurrence of Yellow-browed Warblers and Richard's Pipits — classic western Siberian birds. The further east the birds originate, the later the dates that

A young Rose-coloured Starling on Cape Clear Island, Cork, a bird more commonly encountered in south-east Europe and Turkey *(Victor Caschera)*

they are found in Ireland. Some of the best Sibes are not found in Ireland until the last week of October, or the first week in November.

In the case of the Brown Shrike in Kerry, it didn't turn up until late November. It had travelled in the wrong direction for several months and was now on the very outpost of south-western Ireland. Facing it was the Atlantic Ocean. So what happens to birds like the shrike and the other Sibes? The sad reality is that unless their migratory urge is suppressed, they will probably continue their flight on out into the Atlantic, where they surely perish. Proof that this is the most likely ending for these birds came in 1993 when a Paddyfield Warbler (another eastern species) was found on a fishing boat over 400 km south-west of Ireland. It's not all doom and gloom, however. If they are lucky, some may reach the Canary Islands — in

recent years several Siberian species have been found wintering there. Likewise, a small flock of Richard's Pipits was found in January 1995 in the balmy climes of southern Morocco. A Richard's Pipit has even been found in Ireland in winter.

European species also reverse migrate, of course, which may explain how some of our common migrants find their way to Newfoundland, on the north-east coast of America. One other interesting aspect to the 'reverse migration' theory is that the birds most likely affected by it are those that migrate on a 'west–east' axis as opposed to a 'north–south' axis. In other words, birds that tend to migrate due south from their northerly breeding grounds are less inclined to go the wrong way. This may explain why many migrant birds in North American rarely reverse migrate.

The changing migration habits of Blackcaps mean we now see more in Ireland each winter *(Joe Curtis)*

So is reverse migration serving an actual purpose? Are these birds 'frontier explorers', seeking out new wintering grounds? And if they are successful and return to breed in their usual summer range, will their offspring begin to migrate to the new wintering area? The advantage of this would be known only if there were a natural disaster in the usual wintering grounds. In such an event, the fact that these 'explorers' may have found new wintering areas might actually result in the survival of the species.

Such theories don't have to apply solely to far-distant migrants. In recent years, the number of Blackcaps wintering in Irish gardens has increased significantly. It's believed that these birds come from Germany and Switzerland. Are these the descendants of birds that originally reverse migrated? Did Blackcaps, originally intending to fly south-east to the eastern Mediterranean, actually fly north-west to Ireland? Here they may have enjoyed a food-rich environment and relatively mild winters. Surviving until the following spring, they may have returned to central Europe to breed, before beginning their north-westward migration again in the autumn. Perhaps their young, inheriting the 'wrong' migration instincts, also joined them in Ireland, increasing the numbers occurring here year by year. This is exactly what happened in the case of Blackcaps, and it has been a

very successful tactic for that species. Even more remarkable is recent research that has shown that Blackcaps are now pair-bonding on the wintering grounds before migrating back in spring. That means that Irish wintering birds are breeding only with each other in Europe, but will not breed with Mediterranean-wintering Blackcaps. This ensures that the reverse migration gene is passed on to successive generations.

Migration is a breathtaking natural event. It's one of the greatest spectacles on Earth and has fascinated man for thousands of years. When I see American birds in Ireland, I find it hard not to marvel at the journey they have made. The fact that they have survived their transatlantic flight is a testimony to their instincts and resilience. And when I looked at that Brown Shrike in Dingle on that dull, wet November morning, I didn't see a lost soul. No, instead I felt I was in the presence of a great explorer, pushing out the frontiers for its species. It was last seen on 10 December. Nobody knows where it went. No one saw it leave. I would like to think that it survived and returned to Siberia the following summer. If one or more Brown Shrikes start turning up in Kerry over the next few years, I may, perhaps, have the answer.

Chapter 11

Winter Birdwatching

Snow Bunting *(John Finn)*

It was mid-September and I was out and about. Ireland was enjoying a late burst of summer-like weather. People were still wearing their summer clothes and speaking about the 'fine days we're having'. But I knew something they didn't know.

That morning on the North Bull Island, an extensive mudflat and saltmarsh habitat just outside Dublin City, something was happening. As people strolled by in their light cotton clothes, I knew that things were about to change. There in front of me was a family party of Brent Geese, freshly arrived from their breeding grounds in Arctic Canada to spend the winter in Ireland. To me, these first Brent Geese meant several things: time to root out the winter woollies,

Brent Geese *(Clive Timmons)*

time to put out the nut-feeders in the garden, and a reminder to enjoy the autumn migration while it lasts ... the dark days of winter were just around the corner.

In recent winters I have migrated, like the Swallows, for short breaks. I've visited hot tropical rainforests in South America and travelled across the Namib Desert in Africa. While the landscape, tropical forests, wildlife and birds were breathtaking, my memory is filled with thoughts of scorching sunshine and overbearing heat. It always seems that just as I become acclimatised to a place, it's time to return home. Invariably, I land back in Dublin Airport on a cold, wet winter's day. The sheer joy of such overcast weather is always overwhelming.

Irish winter months, from mid-November to February, should best be viewed in 3-D: it's usually Dull, persistently Damp and, at best, Dreary. But it's precisely this mild 3-D effect that makes Ireland such a fabulous place for birdwatching in wintertime. Our climate is dominated by the mild Atlantic weather systems and as a result of this, we rarely suffer the harsh winter weather that grips our European neighbours each year. Our comparatively mild winters provide rich, soft feeding for thousands of waders, while our wet climate creates the necessary wetlands for countless wildfowl. As well as that, our relatively snow-free weather provides ideal wintering grounds for migrant thrushes and finches, while our resident

Black-tailed Godwit (Anthony McGeehan)

species enjoy a lower winter mortality rate than those on mainland Europe. Also, lying on the western edge of Europe, Ireland is ideally located to attract waders, wildfowl and passerines from breeding grounds in Arctic Canada, Greenland, Iceland, northern Europe and Siberia.

Living in Dublin, I consider myself very lucky to have places like the North Bull Island so close by. Some 20,000 waders, including Black and Bar-tailed Godwits, Knot and Dunlin, winter here each year. Feeding alongside the waders are Brent Geese and ducks, including Teal, Wigeon, Pintail, Shoveler and Shelduck. The sight of such a variety of birdlife within a European capital city is unique and always spectacular. On the south side of Dublin is the vast expanse of Sandymount Strand, with equal numbers of birds. Visiting these mudflats approximately one hour before high tide affords the best opportunity for seeing the birds because they are forced closer to the shore as the water rises.

Further south, the Wexford Wildfowl Reserve holds half the world's population of Greenland White-fronted Geese, along with large numbers of Whooper Swans. The smaller Bewick's Swan has become a much rarer winter visitor to Ireland in recent years, but there is no need for concern about this dramatic population decline. Bewick's Swan breed in northern Russia and Siberia, and in order to reach Ireland, have

Whooper Swans *(Annette Cutts)*

Wigeon, Teal and gulls *(Anthony McGeehan)*

Red-throated Diver *(Adrian Dancy)*

to migrate over Britain. It now seems that there are so many excellent reserves in Britain where the birds can find food and safety, they don't need to travel any further west. Why would they bother to fly across the Irish Sea when they have all the food they need there? Ireland's more remote islands and coastal grasslands of western and north-western regions attract large skeins of Barnacle Geese. These attractive birds fly in from their breeding grounds in Greenland to spend the winter here.

Inland, Ireland's flooded callows and marshes are extremely bird-rich wetland areas. Of these, the Shannon Callows between Portumna in Galway and Athlone in Westmeath, the Little Brosna of Offaly and Tipperary, and the callows of the River Suck in Galway and Roscommon hold important wintering populations of Wigeon and Whooper Swans, along with large numbers of waders, including Golden Plover, Lapwing, Curlew, Black-tailed Godwit and Snipe. Ireland also has a series of large, relatively shallow inland lakes, which are ideal for diving duck. In winter, Lough Neagh and Lough Beg in counties

Antrim, Armagh, Derry and Tyrone together hold the largest numbers of Goldeneye, Pochard and Tufted Duck to be found anywhere in Europe. When visiting such wetlands, always keep to cover — many of these birds are shot and if you break cover, they might just fly.

Along our northern coasts, Snow Buntings can be found feeding on the shingle beaches, while offshore, seaduck, such as Eider and Common Scoter, gather in large flocks. Mixed in with these flocks you may find smaller numbers of Velvet Scoters and Long-tailed Ducks. Our extensive bays and harbours also play host to Great-crested Grebes, Red-throated and Great Northern Divers, while Black Guillemots are a common sight, bedecked in their grey winter plumage.

But enough of all this beautiful scenery … winter also finds me at 'smelly' fishing ports, wandering around depressing docklands and, when possible, on rubbish dumps. It's time for a confession: I'm a gull fanatic. I feel better already having admitted to that. In my travels, I've visited many countries where only one or two species of gull occurs. How, I ask myself,

Black Guillemots in winter plumage *(Breffni Martin)*

Short-eared Owl *(John Finn)*

could I possibly live in these countries without the variety of gulls and the constant challenge in their identification? No, you are all welcome to tropical rainforests and glorious sunshine. Give me a cold winter's day in the docklands of Galway City in western Ireland, where it's not uncommon to see twelve species of gull in a single day.

Birds like Mediterranean Gulls and Little Gulls are my lifeblood, and in winter there's the so-called 'northern gulls' to be found, including aggressive monsters called Glaucous Gulls and the gentler, more attractive Iceland Gull. These white-winged 'northern gulls' breed in Iceland, Greenland and Arctic Canada and occur throughout all coastal counties each winter, with the highest concentrations being in counties Donegal and Galway. Ireland is also occasionally graced with the elegance and beauty of a Ross's Gull. This dainty species breeds in Arctic regions of Siberia, Canada and Greenland and is a rare, but welcome, visitor to Irish coasts.

In the last ten years, Ireland has seen a large increase in the number of wintering Mediterranean

Gulls. We have small numbers of these handsome birds breeding each summer in Ireland, but the majority of wintering birds arrive in autumn from their breeding grounds in the Netherlands and Belgium. The largest wintering concentrations are found at Sandycove in Dublin and around Cobh in Cork (what is it about the word cove/cobh that attracts Mediterranean Gulls?). Occasionally, up to 50 individuals can be seen at any one time. Fishing ports such as Killybegs in Donegal always attract big gull numbers in winter and if visiting Galway, Nimmo's Pier is a must.

Ireland is also an important refuge for many thousands of birds that move westwards to escape extremely cold and harsh winter weather in Europe. Skylarks, Meadow Pipits and colourful finches called Bramblings, along with waders and wildfowl, swell the wintering bird populations. Fortunately, our rich winter food resources seem to cope adequately with these influxes. During such 'hard weather movements', it is possible to witness mass arrivals of birds along our coasts, many near a point of sheer exhaustion having endured a long, hard flight on reduced fat reserves. They make easy pickings for raptors such as Merlin, Peregrine Falcon and Hen Harrier, which move down to the coast each winter from their mountainous breeding areas to avail of the plentiful food supply. Short-eared Owls, a rare breeding bird here in Ireland, are also not uncommon along coastal marshes in winter, with birds arriving in autumn from Iceland, northern Europe and Scotland.

I must now come clean and admit that it's my own garden that provides the most satisfying birding for me each winter. I have a bird-friendly garden, with *Pyracantha* and *Cotoneaster* bushes and native Mountain Ash planted everywhere. By late autumn, they are laden with berries, ready for the winter-feeding. Blackbirds and Mistle Thrushes, along with Redwings and Fieldfares (migrant winter thrushes from northern Europe), will have cleared these bushes and trees clean of their berries by the end of the winter. A small pond or birdbath is also a good addition to a garden; birds need to be able to drink and bathe. Finally, add some nut-feeders and a well-stocked bird table, and your garden will be transformed into a bird-feeding station. Birds are not too fussy, and will eat most things but the one thing you should never put out for them is salted peanuts.

The winter is also the best time to think about erecting a nest-box. Choose a location that is not exposed to direct sunlight … it can get very hot in there in summer. Ideally, your nest-box should be facing east or north; never south or west. By February, birds like Blue Tits will begin checking it out and laying claim to it.

Each autumn, I always smile when I hear people speak of how much they dread the shortening days and the approach of winter. Me, I welcome and enjoy the winter months. It's the best time to go birdwatching in Ireland. What better time to go out and see the wealth of birdlife we have in our wetlands and along our hedgerows. Better still, what better time to settle down at home, dry and warm, and look out at the rain that is falling in a steady downpour in the garden outside. In winter, your garden is full of birds. They don't mind the rain … so why should you?

Fieldfare *(Warren Hewitt)*

Chapter 12

The Language of Birders

A 'Rockit' *(Mícheál Casey)*

In 1981, I was in Ballycotton, in Cork, with a small group of birders. We were down from Dublin to see some wonderful species that had arrived in on southerly winds. I saw my first Little Egret in Ireland,

A 'Little Egger' *(Eric Dempsey)*

as well as Purple Heron, Glossy Ibis and breeding Bearded Tits (or Bearded Reedlings, as they are now known). We were booked into a nice B&B and everything was set for a great weekend. There was one major problem, however. One of the drivers suddenly realised that he had left his wallet behind. I overheard a conversation between him and his close friend. He had no money — what could he do? The answer was easy — he could 'hit his runners early for sting'. It was a perfect solution. His runners were duly hit for sting and everything was sorted!

Later, it dawned on me that had they listened in on that conversation, most people would not have had a clue what was being said. So what did 'hitting runners early for sting' mean? Quite simply, not everyone had a car in the 1980s and for those without one who wanted to experience the best birding, it was vital to befriend an active birder who did drive. You might get offered an occasional trip if someone else opted out, but slowly you graduated to being offered first choice for a birding trip. Sometimes you needed to prove yourself worthy, capable of contributing to the trip by finding some good birds, before being elevated to such dizzy heights. However, once you became an established first-choice passenger with a driver, you were now officially a 'runner' in their car. Of course, there were benefits for the driver. It meant that the cost of the petrol was shared, with each passenger contributing an equal amount of money. As a runner, this was your 'sting'. Sting usually wasn't paid until the very end of the trip, so the solution in Cork that June day in 1981 was that the passengers who were travelling with the driver who had forgotten his wallet would pay their share of the petrol money in advance. 'Hitting your runners for early sting' was indeed a perfect solution, don't you agree? In fact, as I write this in the era of the great Celtic Tiger economy, when most young birders buy cars before buying binoculars, I realise that perhaps such language would equally baffle many modern birders. This was our language in the late 1970s and 1980s and, as with everything, language evolves with time.

Over the years, I've reached a conclusion that birders are occasionally a little like Parisians — they will engage with great enthusiasm if you attempt to speak their language. However, if you insist on speaking your own language and do not even attempt to converse with them in theirs, you'll quickly find yourself being cold-shouldered. Like all languages, it takes some time to become fluent, and birders will quickly spot those who are fluent and those who are struggling. It's even worse to pretend to be fluent … you'll be quickly found out. To be fluent, you need to think in the language of birders. It's a major undertaking to translate this language fully for laypeople, but I'll attempt in some way to give a quick lesson in speaking 'birder'.

At the very outset, there is one general rule: birders always shorten words and use abbreviations. Let's face it, who wants to be wasting breath and time on long words when there is birding to be done? For that reason we are 'birders' and not 'birdwatchers'. We go 'birding' and not 'birdwatching'. Most people will understand the term 'birdwatching', so you may need to describe yourself as a birdwatcher. This is perfectly acceptable under many circumstances, such as when you are speaking to a landowner on whose land is a bird that you would like to see. In that kind of situation, seeing the bird comes first, and it's quite admirable to describe yourself in whatever way it takes to see the bird. However, under no circumstances should you ever accept being referred to as a 'bird fancier' — that is a step too far. In his *Little Black Bird Book,* Bill Oddie suggests that the terms 'birding' and 'birder' give a more rugged and outdoors feel to the pursuit and I do agree with him on that. It seems that you start off as a birdwatcher and end up a birder. It is worth noting that in the USA, everyone is a birder and goes birding; no one is a birdwatcher and no one goes birdwatching. Another interesting and intriguing difference between the two continents is the fact that there are more women birders in the USA than in Europe, where it's predominantly a male pursuit.

Having the right equipment is essential for birding, but knowing what to call this equipment is

'BallyC', Co. Cork *(Sean Cronin)*

equally important. Just like the activity itself, the equipment used also has abbreviated names. Hence we use 'bins' and not 'binoculars'.

When you really get into birding, it eventually becomes obvious that a good telescope is the next step. Choosing the right one is more important than choosing the right partner in life. Some of your best moments in life will be spent with this piece of equipment, so choose well and wisely. Regardless of the make or size, always refer to it as a 'scope', never as a 'telescope'. Having a scope with you shows that you've made a commitment to birding and that you're serious about it. That is, as long as you're not carrying a giant astronomical telescope. While these may be ideal for looking at the moon, try using it to follow a feeding wader on a mudflat among thousands of others and you'll soon realise just how inadequate they are for birding. Of course, there are some superb astronomical scopes that will allow you to see such waders at great distances, but these are usually very expensive and sometimes difficult to use. Some birders have them as back-ups to their normal scopes, but will use them only when trying to see something very far away. Carrying two scopes will certainly do wonders for your 'street cred'. A tripod is also an essential piece of equipment (you can't use your scope without one). Your tripod is simply referred to as a 'pod'. Many birders are also using digital cameras along with their scopes. By using a simple little adapter, some cameras can be attached to the scope, which acts like a big telephoto lens. This new form of bird photography is called 'digi-scoping' and many people get wonderful images using this technique.

So, having the right equipment is an important step for anyone starting off and will gain you some instant respect from other birders. Your bins and scope are status symbols, but regardless of the make of bins or scope you choose, if you wish to retain some level of respect, always remember to refer to them correctly. As you become more fluent in 'birder', you can even change the meanings of the words themselves. For example, the noun 'scope' can instantly become a verb when you 'scope' through a flock of waders. You can also 'digi-scope' a bird, but always remember that you can never 'bin' a bird with bins!

Armed with a firm basic knowledge of how to refer to your activity and your equipment, it's time to venture out to the various birding locations. Like everything else, the names of these places are also abbreviated. One easy rule to follow is that if the place name includes the word island, drop the word 'island'. Hence we visit 'Tory' and 'Dursey', rather than Tory Island and Dursey Island. If the island has a double-barrelled name, drop the second part as well, making Cape Clear Island 'Cape' and the North Bull Island

'Rog', Co. Dublin (*Victor Caschera*)

simply 'the Bull'. Likewise with headlands — drop the word 'Head' from all the names to give locations like 'Hook', 'Brownstown' and 'Galley'. The Old Head of Kinsale is the exception. In birder, this is simply known as the 'Old Head'. Dropping sections from place names implies a familiarity with them and helps you appear wise and widely travelled. It's so easy to do … Ballycotton is 'BallyC', Rogerstown Estuary is 'Rog' and Tacumshin Lake is 'Tackers'.

However, let me offer a word of caution about using these abbreviations too quickly. Many of the areas above also have special birding locations within them. For example, Hook has lots of gardens and laneways, and knowing them is an essential part of speaking fluently. There is Slade Lane, Fortune's Lane, Lupin Cottage, the Honey Pot Garden and Lark Cottage, to name but a few. So if you're boasting about seeing birds on Hook, it's essential to mention a few place names within Hook in order to get away with it successfully. Likewise, Galley has Marsh Lane, Shite Lane and Dirk Bay, while Tackers has the East

End, the Forgotten Corner, the Patches and the White Hole. Some areas are even named after birds that have been seen there. On Cape is a small valley that leads up from the West Bog called 'Olly Gully', named after an Olivaceous Warbler that spent a few days there (which in fact turned out to be Ireland's first Syke's Warbler, but that's another story). Becoming familiar with the best birding locations is worthwhile and prepares you for the most important step in speaking birder … learning what to call the birds themselves.

To be able to speak this language fluently requires a firm understanding of birds because, like everything else in birding, bird names are frequently abbreviated. Being able to shorten bird names accurately reflects the experience you have in the field. Some names are easy. For example, Manx Shearwaters become 'Manxies' and Storm Petrels become 'Stormies'. These are easy because you won't come across any other bird names that start with the words 'Manx' or 'Storm'. There are many species like this and the instant way to abbreviate them is by

'Stormies' (Anthony McGeehan)

Little Grebe, NOT a 'Dabchick' (John Finn)

simply dropping the last part of their name. To be able to do this successfully, however, you need to know that some species share a first name. For example, in the world of grebes, we can drop the word 'grebe' from Black-necked Grebe. We can even shorten Slavonian Grebe to 'Slav', but we always give Little Grebe its full name. Why? Well, if we say that we saw a 'Little', what exactly are we referring to? A Little Egret, Little Stint or Little Gull? Likewise Little Egrets, Stints and Gulls are also afforded full name status. By the way, it's not cool to refer to Little Grebes as 'Dabchicks'.

Therefore the first step in speaking this language is to simply drop the last part of the name when you can. As you become more fluent, you can abbreviate names further. Wader-watchers have become very adept at this. So, American Golden Plovers become 'AGPs', Pacific Golden Plovers are 'PGPs' and Little Ringed Plovers, 'LRPs'. However, Buff-breasted Sandpipers are not 'BBs' but 'Buff-bs'. That is because there is a bird called a Broad-billed Sandpiper … another BB, which could cause confusion. When a

bird does share the first part of its name with another species, the compromise is to try to shorten the second part, if you can. Hence we have 'Curlew' and 'Curlew S' ('S' being short for 'Sandpiper'). In some cases, both parts of the name can be abbreviated, resulting in 'Spotty Fly' (for Spotted Flycatcher) and 'Spotty Red' (for Spotted Redshank).

In the world of gulls, you can become even more fluent and display your wonderful grasp of the language. Lesser Black-backed Gulls become 'LBBs' while Mediterranean Gulls are known as 'Meds'. Understanding the ageing process of the gulls will allow you to attain new heights. If asked, 'Have you seen anything with the gull flocks?' ... replying 'Four Meds' is a perfect answer. However, by quickly adding, 'a first-winter, two second-winters and an adult' you will show just how fluent you are in birder. If you really want to impress, the best answer to that question would be 'Just four Meds'. The use of the word 'just' implies that you're so experienced, seeing four Mediterranean Gulls doesn't impress you at all

'LRP' *(Adrian Dancy)*

An 'AGP' *(Paul Kelly)*

(even if moments before you've been jumping for joy at seeing them for the very first time).

Having knowledge of the scientific names for birds or their families is better still. That way, you don't even have to bother with species names. On a headland in autumn or spring, you may see Chiffchaffs (Chiffers) and Willow Warblers (Willows). These species belong to the *Phylloscopus* group of warblers. Being able to refer to these confidently as 'Phylloscs' shows that you're not only familiar with the birds but also their Latin names. This is speaking birder fluently. It's even better if you know the Latin names for races of birds. A perfect example of this is the humble Herring Gull. The scientific name for Herring Gulls is *Larus argentatus*. There are many different races of Herring Gull, but the one that occurs in Ireland and Britain is *Larus argentatus 'argenteus'*. Birds from Scandinavia are of the race *Larus argentatus 'argentatus'*. To know this fact is impressive to start with, but being able to recognise one when you see one is even more so. By referring to these birds in conversation simply as 'argies' is to elevate your language skills to new heights.

Occasionally you may catch a glimpse of a bird that you cannot identify, or that you haven't seen well enough to be certain of its identity. If you don't see it again, this bird becomes a 'hoodwink'. Hoodwinks are very annoying — they give you a tantalising moment of excitement before they disappear for good, leaving you pondering on the possibilities of what might have been. If that hoodwink is a small, brownish bird, then it is given the status of an LBJ (Little Brown Job). Being able to speak fluently about what you haven't seen is just as important as being able to speak fluently about what you have seen!

Many birders also use slang words for birds, with Grasshopper Warblers becoming 'Groppers', Blackcaps becoming 'Caps', Rock and Meadow Pipits

An 'argi' *(Derek Charles)*

A 'Mipit' *(Tom Cuffe)*

becoming 'Rockits' and 'Mipits' respectively, while Black-tailed and Bar-tailed Godwits are frequently relegated to 'Black-wits' and 'Bar-wits'. Little Egrets are also known as 'Little Eggers' (which isn't shortened at all but gives a feeling of familiarity). Of course, there are many bird names that are not abbreviated. These are birds that usually have short names to start with: Dunnocks are Dunnocks, Robins are Robins and Dippers will always be Dippers.

Speaking of Dippers … no birder ever wants to be a 'dipper'. Dipping is a dreadful experience, to be avoided at all costs. Sometimes it can take years to get over the experience and, in some unfortunate cases, birders may never get over dipping at all. Let me explain. When you start birding, you usually find yourself keeping tabs on what you've seen. This is known as 'keeping a list'. You can keep a garden list, a county list or even a car list. Put simply, this is a list of all the bird species you have seen in your garden, in

Two vintage Irish 'ticks' — Pied Wheatear at Knockadoon Head in 1980, and American Coot at Ballycotton in 1981 *(Both photos: Richard T. Mills)*

your county or when driving. A friend of mine surfs and keeps a 'surfing list', while another person I know keeps an 'apartment list'. Most people, though, keep just two main lists: a country list (living in Ireland, I have an Irish List) and a life list. My Irish list is a tally of all the bird species I have seen in Ireland since I began birding. My life list is a tally of all the species I have seen throughout the world. When you see a bird for the first time, you get a 'tick'. This term derives from the perception that you simply place a 'tick' against that bird in a book when you've seen it. It also explains why, in the language of birder, you 'get' birds and not 'see' them. If in Wexford you see a Buff-breasted Sandpiper and a Curlew Sandpiper, you will have 'got' a Buff-b and a Curlew S. Many people also keep a 'year list', keeping track of the number of birds they have seen each year. This is usually great fun and on days when things seem quiet, getting a few 'year ticks' will keep you going.

For some of us, we may only get two or three ticks each year in Ireland. These may be birds we have seen elsewhere in the world, so they are 'Irish ticks'. Should I see a bird in Ireland that I've never ever seen before, then not only do I get an Irish tick but I also get a 'lifer'. Both my Irish and life lists go up by one. Having a good country list is almost a way of establishing your vintage. In Ireland, having birds like the Knockadoon Head Pied Wheatear (1980) or the Ballycotton American Coot (1981) on your list gives you some form of respectability among your peers. This is not necessarily due to your skills or indeed your knowledge, but is more an acknowledgment of years spent behind the scope. Keeping and comparing lists with others also introduces a friendly rivalry between birders.

Talk of lists can sometimes reduce the art and skill of birding down to that of train-spotting, i.e. merely keeping a tally. But birding is really very different. It is one of the most unpredictable pastimes — you can never know just what you might see when you go out birding. The very fact that birds undertake long migrations means that it is conceivable that almost any bird might turn up in autumn and spring … and you might just be the person to find it. For some, however, the driving force behind their birding is to get ticks and to increase their lists. There are many people who will drop everything at a moment's notice and travel hundreds of kilometres to see a new bird (get a tick). These are known as 'twitchers'. During migration periods, they can travel the length and breadth of the country in pursuit of ticks. And when they see the bird … well, the moment of ticking off a bird is difficult to describe. All the hours of tension and hope have suddenly been worth it. There, assaulting their optic nerves, is the reason for their very existence. It could be a bird that they have wanted to see all of their lives. It may be so rare that they may never again get the opportunity to see this bird, even if they live to be 120 years old. Even better, it may be a bird that their friends (listing rivals) have already seen and, as a result, have been holding one tick over them for years. When this happens, not only do they get an Irish tick and a lifer, but they are also getting a 'catch-up'.

However, there is one big problem with travelling to see rare birds: they have wings (have wings, will fly). There really is nothing worse than travelling hundreds of kilometres throughout the night to arrive at a remote headland for dawn only to find that the bird that you wanted to see (a tick) has flown off during the night. When this happens, you experience the horrible sensation of 'dipping'. No one wants to dip. Dippers experience nightmares, waking up screaming at night. We have all dipped. I missed Ireland's second ever record of a Baltimore Oriole by the width of a branch. While birders beside me could see this beautiful North American bird, a branch was blocking my view. By the time I moved, the bird had flown and never showed itself again while I was there. I dipped badly. You need to be philosophical about these things, though, otherwise you'll never survive. You may even dip many times when trying to see a certain species. When this happens, that species becomes your 'bogey bird'. It can often take years to finally catch-up on a bogey bird, but needless to say, it is particularly satisfying when you do.

Dipping is bad enough, but when you meet someone who has seen the bird and who insists on rubbing salt into your wounds by telling you how wonderful an experience it was, then you find yourself being 'gripped off'. People who grip you off are not nice people. They seem to have forgotten how dreadful dipping can be. They have lost their humanity. The one consolation you have is that you know it will only be a matter of time before they too dip on something. What goes around, comes around.

There are some people who claim they never twitch, but if a rare bird is found only 300 m away from where they live, they will of course go and see it. The only difference between them and the 'hardcore twitchers' is that the latter are prepared to travel 300 km to see the same bird. Let's face it, we're all twitchers at heart. We all like to get a tick every now and then!

Of course, in order to twitch a bird, it must be found in the first place. Finding a major rarity (a 'mega') is perhaps one of the most enriching

The Canada Warbler, found on Loop Head, Co. Clare
(Michael O'Keeffe)

experiences of your birding life. It will earn you a place in birding lore and, depending on the bird, you can live off the kudos for years (or sometimes for the rest of your life). Finding a species never before seen in the country or even in Europe will elevate you to celebrity status. The real joy in finding rare birds is in sharing that information with as many people as possible, affording them the opportunity to twitch it. However, there are times when there are good reasons why information needs to be withheld from other birders. Perhaps the bird is breeding and undue human activity might disturb it, or it might be on private property. Both are understood and accepted by birders as valid and acceptable reasons for not sharing the information.

Unfortunately, there are some birders who simply don't like sharing their finds with anyone. There is no reason other than they want to keep the pleasure all to themselves. These are the dreaded breed of birder known as 'suppressors'. Suppressing a find is a mortal sin in the world of birders and twitchers, particularly if it's a deliberate act simply to prevent others from seeing a bird. Suppressors seem to derive as much pleasure from gripping off their fellow birders as they do in seeing rare birds. Suppressors are even worse if they travel to see other people's finds. If news of their suppression gets out, they will quickly find themselves isolated within the birding family. That is the price to be paid for being a suppressor.

There is another dreaded 'S' word in the world of birding, and it's the very kudos associated with finding a rare bird that can draw this particular kind of birder out of the woodwork. These are the reviled 'stringers'. There are unwritten rules between birders.

Twitchers watching the Canada Warbler at Loop Head the morning after its discovery. Many had travelled overnight from all over Ireland and Britain *(Victor Caschera)*

There is a sacred trust. It would be easy to claim to have seen a rare bird, tell everyone about it, and then announce it had flown away before anyone else can see it. In real life this happens — birds do fly away and not all birds found will stay long enough for others to see. When this happens, you have to take the person's word for it. You need to trust them that they have indeed seen the bird and are not stringing you along. In most cases, this trust is a given. Stringers are those birders who frequently claim to see rare birds that others somehow never see. Hoodwinks and LBJs don't exist for them; everything is identified. They will tell the world and its family about their finds, but invariably the bird flies before anyone gets there. Being labelled a stringer is the worst possible thing for a birder. Once labelled, that birder, regardless of whatever they achieve in life, will go to their grave as a stringer, and their descendants for the next 50 generations will always be under suspicion. They have broken the sacred trust among birders and that is never forgotten.

People do make mistakes, of course, and while it can be frustrating for twitchers to travel for hours to see a bird that has been genuinely misidentified, if the finder accepts the mistake and owns up to it, then there is never any problem. It has happened to us all. Let he who is without sin cast the first stone and all that. In fact, when this happens, the finder gains more respect among the birding fraternity for being so honest. Stringers would never own up to such errors. If they claim to see a bird and lots of birders arrive, only to discover that in the exact place where the rare bird is supposed to be is a very similar species (and one that is frequently mistaken for the claimed rarer bird), then the stringer instantly falls back on the famous 'Two Bird Theory'. The stringer will claim that there were two birds present, the rare one and the frequently mistaken one, but — surprise, surprise — the rare one has flown off. Thankfully, in the age of digi-scoping, it is becoming increasingly difficult for stringers to claim to have had good views of a bird before it flew, especially when everyone knows they have a camera. If a rare bird gives good views, then surely a stringer could manage to take one shot of it?

Even if the image is not perfect, it is at least an undeniable record of the bird's existence. In birding, this is called a 'record shot', and many rare birds have been accepted as genuine based on such photos.

In recent years, I've come to realise that birders also like to torment one another. There are many people who go out birding when they know everyone else is stuck at work. This is known as 'sniping'. 'Snipers' (yet another S word) ply their trade in one of two ways. Some will go birding in the hope of finding rare birds without people even knowing that they are out and about. Others prefer to tell everyone that they are going birding in the knowledge that other birders may spend the day wondering what, if anything, they may find. This works very well in favourable weather conditions during the migration seasons. The key is that if they do find something good, everyone will be told and the sniper has struck again. There are some birders who are such well-renowned snipers that their Christian names have now been replaced by the word 'Sniper'.

Of course, there are millions of people who rightly choose to have no interest in birds. Such people are sometimes referred to as 'dudes'. This is a rather derogatory term, and I much prefer how a friend of mine refers to non-birders. He calls them 'civilians'. Birders and civilians get on very well in life as long as their paths don't cross at critical times. If you're out birding and a busload of people arrive, disturbing the flocks of birds you've been scoping, then those civilians very quickly become 'dudes'. Many a day's birding has been ruined by a busload of dudes!

Being a birder and speaking 'birder' fluently is a joy and a wonderful asset. Learn the language, converse freely, but always remember, in the immortal words of Shakespeare:

Neither a suppressor nor a stringer be;
For suppressing oft loses both itself and friend,
And stringing dulls the edge of twitchery.
This above all: to thine own list be true,
And it must follow, as the night the day,
Thou canst not then be false to any man.

Chapter 13

Splitters and Lumpers

Races of Dunlin — *alpina* left, *arctica* right *(Martin Garner)*

In the birding world of today, we're delighted when we hear that a major split is on the way. It gives us all an 'armchair tick'. Those who advocate splitting are everyone's friends. Lumpers, on the other hand, are not liked at all. They are the pedantic spoilsports of the birding community.

Is this a Mute Swan or a Whooper Swan? Actually, it's both *(Eric Dempsey)*

No doubt you're scratching your head at this point and wondering what I'm talking about. Put simply, I'm referring to the new science of splitting races of birds into distinct species, or the cruel act of deciding that two species are in fact mere races of the same species (lumping them together). This raises the important question: what makes a species a species? When is a bird a species and when is it a race (or a subspecies, as they are often called — both terms mean the same thing)?

To understand the difference, let us look at the meanings of both words in human terms. The scientific name for our species is *Homo sapiens* — we are human beings. This method of naming species was created by the 18th century Swedish naturalist, Carl von Linné (Linnaeus in Latin). The first section is the genus name; the second is the species name. This name is usually in Latin (although some names are of Greek origin) and is known as the Linnaean name. We belong to the Class of Mammals and the Order of Primates. Other members of the Order include Chimpanzees, Orang-utans and Gorillas. We are four distinct species, but closely related to one another. We do not interbreed, even in areas where our populations overlap. Even if we did attempt to interbreed, we are genetically so different that any young produced would be infertile. We behave differently and communicate in different ways. These differences are what defines us as distinct species from the other

White Wagtail. Split it or lump it? *(Mícheál Casey)*

Pied Wagtail *(Sean Cronin)*

primates and what also defines them as different from us and each other. This is what is known as the Biological Species Concept (or BSC for short).

However, within the human species, there are many different varieties according to the region where humans are found. In central Africa, for example, members of our species are very dark-skinned with dark eyes and dark hair. In Europe, humans along the Mediterranean coast have paler skin than Africans and also usually have brown eyes and black hair. Further north in Europe, Scandinavians are known for their pale skin, blonde hair and pale blue eyes. In Asia, many other varieties occur, from those found in India to those of China and Mongolia. While each group is quite distinctive, where populations overlap, successful breeding takes place, producing fertile offspring. I know this all sounds very impersonal, but for the purposes of the subject-matter, it shows one thing: despite the apparent differences between human beings from different parts of the world, biologically and genetically we are the same species. The differences that occur between us, such as skin colour, eye colour, features or hair colour, simply define each group as a race within our species.

Now let us apply that to birds. Take the Pied Wagtail, for example. Pied Wagtails occur in many areas of the northern hemisphere and appear quite different from each other. The birds that occur in Ireland are very black on the back and rump, while those found in Iceland and northern Europe are pale grey (and are known as White Wagtails). Others, occurring in Siberia, show a unique pattern of black on the face. In fact, there are at least ten races of Pied/White Wagtail (the species is actually known as White Wagtail; only the race that occurs in Ireland and Britain is known as Pied Wagtail). Despite these differences, where the populations of these different wagtail races overlap, the birds interbreed and produce fertile young. Just like human beings, the differences that occur between them simply define each group as a race within the species. In effect, each race has evolved to appear different from other races, but has not evolved quite far enough to be considered a separate species. To put it another way, if isolated from each other, races are considered to be species in

A hybrid Goosander x Eider — one you won't find in the field guide (Martin Garner)

The Irish race of Coal Tit is yellower than the British and European races *(Sean Cronin)*

Herring Gull — one species, or 15? *(Eric Dempsey)*

the making. There are several other black-and-white wagtail species, but even where the population of these birds overlaps with those of Pied/White Wagtail, they never interbreed. This is the Biological Species Concept at work.

So, is that it when it comes to what makes a species a species? Up until relatively recently, the answer to that question was 'yes'. But things have changed. With the development of genetic finger-printing (or genetic bar-coding, as it's sometimes known), the traditional theories and understandings of species definitions (speciation) have been thrown on their head. New ways of defining species have been developed that are quite revolutionary. In short, some now believe that the only true way of defining a species is by examining the genetic make-up of a bird or a mammal. This new way of defining species is known as the Phylogenetic Species Concept (PSC).

The British race of Coal Tit *(Adrian Dancy)*

The effects of the PSC are quite dramatic and the cutting-edge of this new science is being sharpened on the bird world. The PSC states that if races of birds appear different from each other, and that if those races show different genetic make-ups, then they should be 'split' and considered full species. The best example of this is the Herring Gull. Until recently, there was one species of Herring Gull with the scientific name of *Larus argentatus*. Just like us, Herring Gulls occur all around the northern hemisphere, from North America, Europe and into Asia, and also just like us there were many unique races within the species. Having examined the DNA of all the races of Herring Gull, supporters of the PSC now believe that there are in fact at least 15 different species of gull. Two distinct species (the Herring Gull and Yellow-legged Gull) occur in Ireland each year, with two more also being recorded on occasions. It was recommended by the taxonomic authorities (these are the groups that study such things) that these former races of Herring Gull be accepted as full species in their own right. Overnight, birders in

Ireland were able to add several new species to their lists. As you know, a new species on your list is known as a tick, but when you get a new species on your list as a result of a split, it's known as an 'armchair tick'. For some die-hard BSC supporters, this new approach is as radical as stating that, within Europe, humans who come from Spain are a different species from those who hail from Sweden.

The other problem some people might have with the PSC is that sometimes (although rarely, it must be said), two species of bird are found to have very similar DNA and should actually be considered races, and not species. When this happens, a bird is removed from a person's list as a result of two species being 'lumped' together as one. That is why scientists who discover such things are not very well liked (birders really do hate lumpers).

So, is the PSC being used as the new species definition process? This is where the whole issue begins to get muddied. Within Europe, there are two lines of thought within the scientific and taxonomic communities. There are those who prefer the more traditional methods of BSC and those who support the PSC. In the Netherlands, for example, races of Pied/White Wagtails are recognised as full species, but here in Ireland they are still considered to be races. In the USA, more and more species are being split, while on this side of the Atlantic, the same birds are still being considered as races. It has also thrown up some interesting species. According to the PSC, there are several species of Chiffchaff. They all look the same, but their calls are different. The fact that the calls are unique and that the birds are genetically different must prove something, but where is the defining line between race and species when it comes to Chiffchaffs? Have the races of Chiffchaff evolved to such a point where they are now full species? This is, of course, the big question and as the science is so new, it seems many are reluctant to embrace it. On the other hand, others have embraced it fully and seem to have forgotten the old BSC.

Are there any advantages to elevating a race of bird to the status of a full species? From the bird's point of view, it really makes no difference. They know if a bird they encounter is potentially a breeding

Races of Chiffchaff have been the subject of several recent 'splits' *(Richard T. Mills)*

partner. It seems that the fact of whether a bird is a race or a species only matters to us humans, who like to categorise things neatly into boxes or who like to be able to add a species to a list. But there is one important element in which a species seems to hold more sway than a race. That is when it comes to conservation. It seems our political masters are always more interested in saving a species from extinction, but are never really too bothered about saving a race. For that reason, many conservationists are beginning to support the PSC, with more and more species being recognised and, as a result, being afforded full species protection.

For some purists, the BSC is the only way, but perhaps the truth lies in a compromise between the two schools of thought. Regardless, if a race of bird enjoys better environmental protection as a result of it being upgraded to a full species, then where is the harm in that? Spilt them all, I say! Now, I'll just sit back in my big, comfy armchair and watch my life list grow.

Chapter 14

Here Today, Gone Tomorrow?

Collared Dove *(Sean Cronin)*

On a recent day's birding in Dublin, I counted no fewer than 40 Little Egrets at various locations around the county. That's no big deal for Irish birders nowadays, but looking through my old notebooks, I realised that I only saw my first ever Little Egret in Ireland in 1981. I had travelled down to Ballycotton,

A male Bearded Tit, part of a small colony at Ballycotton in the 1980s *(Richard T. Mills)*

in Cork, specifically to see this major rarity. Now these exotic white herons no longer even raise an eyebrow, with hundreds of breeding pairs ranging from the coastal counties of Louth to Kerry. They are also being seen inland. Ironically enough, on that same trip to Ballycotton all those years ago, I also saw five Bearded Tits (Bearded Reedlings), part of the breeding colony that existed there. Several years later, a severe winter exterminated that colony and others along the east coast. In one winter, Bearded Tits were no longer in Ireland. If someone had told me on that June day in 1981 that Little Egrets would be breeding in Ireland and Bearded Tits would be gone, I simply would not have believed them.

The lesson I have since learned is that bird populations are not stable and a whole range of factors, from habitat loss, changes in farming practices to climate change, can have dramatic effects on our birdlife. Bird populations can also explode for no apparent reason — you only have to look at Collared Doves to prove this point. It's hard to believe that this now common bird was first recorded in Ireland in 1959. Prior to 1930, this species bred in distant countries like Turkey, Albania and Bulgaria. From the 1930s onwards, the population expanded westwards, until the birds finally reached our shores. This westward expansion is continuing, with Collared Doves now found in some east coast US states in the last few years.

Such changes in population dynamics are not just a recent phenomenon. This is confirmed by examining the first recorded Irish bird observations, which were made by Welsh monk Giraldus Cambrensis in his *History and Topography of Ireland*, compiled in the 12th century. In this epic work, he refers to birds such as Ospreys as 'common', while also referring to the absence of Magpies in Ireland. In fact, the good old Magpie wasn't seen in Ireland until a small population arrived into Wexford in the 1670s … they certainly have done very well since. Giraldus also referred to Golden Eagles as being 'as numerous as kites are in other countries'. Birds of prey populations, in particular, have changed significantly over the last 200 years. Eminent ornithologists of the 19th century, such as Thompson (1849), mention that White-tailed Eagles were 'found in suitable coastal locations throughout Ireland', while Watters (1853) referred to birds like Marsh Harrier as being the 'most abundant of our larger birds of prey'. The last pair of White-tailed Eagles was most likely seen in Mayo in the late 1880s. The great sadness is that all of these magnificent raptors were lost to Ireland as breeding species not because of some natural event or change but as a direct result of human persecution. Gamekeepers and farmers poisoned, shot or trapped these birds out of existence. For example, in Horn Head, Donegal, a gamekeeper proudly boasted that in the late 1820s he had shot 13 White-tailed Eagles in four years — what chance did these birds have?

Given a chance, however, raptors will recover. Peregrine Falcons were almost exterminated in the 1960s when the poison DDT was used as an insecticide. Pigeons ate grain infected with large levels of DDT. It didn't really affect them, but pigeons are the Peregrines' favourite prey. These superb falcons inadvertently ingested vast quantities of poison. So when the females laid eggs, the eggshells were so thin they broke their eggs when attempting to incubate them. When this was discovered, the use of DDT was controlled and the falcon population did recover. Further control on the use of poisons has resulted in the southern expansion of Buzzards as a breeding species in Ireland. These handsome birds are

Magpies didn't reach Ireland until around 1670 *(Eric Dempsey)*

now spreading across the country and should be welcomed by the farming communities for their ability to keep crow, rabbit and rat populations in check.

It has been controls on the use of poisons as well as the co-operation between farming organisations and conservation bodies that have paved the way for the re-introduction of Golden Eagles into Donegal. Almost 50 birds have been released into the wild, and in 2005 a pair attempted to breed. The young female laid an infertile egg, but it was the first Golden Eagle egg laid in the wild in Ireland in 45 years. In 2007, the first Golden Eagle chick hatched successfully. That same year, re-introduction programmes saw White-tailed Eagles once again soaring wild and free in Kerry and Red Kites gracing the skies of Wicklow.

While declines in raptors can be very obvious, other species seem to drift slowly into oblivion, almost un-noticed. Woodlarks are a classic example. This species, smaller than our Skylark and lacking the distinctive crest of the latter, was considered a reasonably widespread breeding bird until the mid-19th century when, for no apparent reason, their numbers plummeted. This decline was paralleled in Britain at the same time. By the turn of the 19th century, they were no longer in Ireland. Hope springs eternal, however, and news from Britain has restored great anticipation that this beautiful lark will soon return. Just as they declined for no apparent reason, it appears that Woodlarks are suddenly enjoying an incredible recovery. In recent years, breeding numbers have increased in Britain from under 50 pairs to over 500, with birds now being seen as close as Wales. I saw my first Woodlark in Ireland in the spring of 2002 and, looking at that bird, I wondered if it would be the first of many I will see over the coming years.

Habitat loss and disturbance are certainly the key factors in the demise of species. Grey Partridges were found in every county in Ireland during the 19th century, but are now restricted to just one small population in the bogs of Offaly. It is believed that fewer than 20 native birds existed at the turn of the 21st century. Pressure from shooting and loss of suitable habitat have been the main culprits for this

An introduced White-tailed Eagle in Kerry *(Valerie O'Sullivan)*

An introduced Golden Eagle in Donegal *(Eddie Dunne)*

Wild Grey Partridges are now confined to just one site in Ireland, in Offaly *(Eddie Dunne)*

species. It's no coincidence that the remaining birds are found on protected boglands. Thankfully, a captive breeding and release programme is paying dividends, with numbers increasing slowly. Nightjars, hawk-like nocturnal birds, are also an extremely rare breeding species. Yet in the 1950s, their strange 'churring' calls could be heard on Howth Head, in the suburbs of Dublin. Each year, small numbers still make it to Ireland and breed in remote forests, but these birds represent the last remnants of a once common summer visitor.

Perhaps the saddest recent breeding extinction is that of the Corn Bunting, a large-billed, pale brown bird that has a very distinctive call, often likened to the sound of 'jangling keys'. It was another foray into my old notebooks that hit home just how recently and quickly some bird species disappear. In June 1991, on a weekend trip to Mayo, I watched a pair of Corn Buntings feeding young. At the same time, I could

hear the distinctive rasping call of a nearby Corncrake. That morning, about 1 km away, I had sat watching a pair of Red-necked Phalaropes (the most southern breeding pair in the world). A return visit in 1992 reflects a significant change in just 12 short months. There were no Corn Buntings to be found, no Corncrakes to be heard, and the marsh where the phalaropes had nested was empty of these diminutive, tame and beautiful wading birds. Up to 50 pairs of Red-necked Phalaropes bred on the marsh in 1923, but numbers declined thereafter, with breeding taking place only occasionally. The reasons why these waders left may be twofold. Perhaps it was unusual for them to be there in the first place and, as the climate warmed, their natural instincts took them to breeding locations much further north, into Iceland. However, the marsh also became very overgrown and unsuitable for the birds, which require small channels of water in which to feed. Work is now taking place to

112

The first Golden Eagle chick to hatch in Ireland in nearly half a century, in Donegal in 2007 *(Lorcan O'Toole)*

restore the marsh and, who knows, perhaps the phalaropes will return some day.

Corn Buntings, on the other hand, are an altogether different story. Once found throughout Ireland, changes in farming techniques have resulted in the loss of suitable feeding habitats for the birds. Without food, the birds simply could not raise young. They were impacted to such an extent that in the late 1990s, they became extinct as a breeding species. This is every bit as dramatic an event as the loss of a large bird of prey and it gives us a major insight into the state of our environment. Nonetheless, the birds' extinction as a breeding species in Ireland barely got a mention in the media. Who was really interested in the demise of a small, rather non-descript brown bird?

It is perhaps the Corncrake that best demonstrates how changes in habitat management and farming techniques can bring a species almost to the brink of extinction. With many farmers abandoning the traditional cutting of hay for the more economically viable use of silage, Corncrakes simply didn't have time to nest and fledge their young before the first cut of grass was made. Many eggs and chicks were destroyed. Fields are usually cut from the outside in, leaving a final swathe in the centre. Stuck in this swathe and reluctant to break cover, the females were killed in the final cut. It seemed all was lost until a conservation programme was launched in the Shannon Callows. These midland grasslands, flooded by the River Shannon each winter, are too wet to cut early in the season. This gives the birds enough time to breed and fledge their young. In addition, grants were offered to delay mowing, allowing birds the chance to breed successfully. Other farmers were encouraged to mow in a 'Corncrake-friendly' manner. This involves cutting grass from the inside out, allowing birds to escape into ditches along the field edges. This programme was very successful, with

Nightjar — now a very rare breeding bird in Ireland *(Tom Shevlin)*

Corncrake numbers increasingly significantly in the 1990s. However, in recent years, numbers of Corncrakes along the Callows have decreased dramatically.

Despite all the conservation work, it seems that climate change is perhaps taking a heavy toll on the success of the species here. Successive wet, early summers have flooded the breeding grounds to such an extent that the high water levels have rendered the area unsuitable for breeding Corncrakes. All is not lost, though. The birds are now re-establishing themselves back in former haunts, like Kerry and Mayo, where their 'crek-crek' calls were long forgotten. On Tory Island in Donegal, Corncrake numbers are at their highest levels for years. This is

not just good for the birds; it is providing a new eco-tourist industry for the island.

While much of the above may make for very depressing reading, nature does have a way of balancing things out. While many species have been lost to us as breeding species, many have also joined our native breeding avifauna. I've already mentioned the success story of the Little Egret, and they are not alone. Walk into a large reedbed in the south or southeast region in summer and you'll no doubt hear the sharp notes of Reed Warblers (rather plain brown-and-white birds) alongside the Sedge Warblers. These first bred in Cork in 1979 and have since colonised reedbeds throughout the south and east coasts. They have also firmly established themselves in some northern counties. Mediterranean Gulls, once a rare winter visitor, are now breeding in very small numbers. The breeding success stories are not just confined to southern species either. Birds that bred no closer than the northern isles of Scotland and Iceland

Gone but not forgotten. Corn Bunting is now extinct in Ireland *(John Finn)*

Fan-tailed Warbler — a future colonist?
(Anthony McGeehan)

Audouin's Gull — another future addition to our birdlife?
(Anthony McGeehan)

are now breeding in Ireland. For example, Whooper Swans, usually considered a winter visitor, established a small breeding population in Donegal in the mid-1990s and have reared young there every year since. Seabirds called Great Skuas (or 'Bonxies', as they are sometimes called) bred in Ireland for the first time in 2001. The pair successfully raised two young. Another winter visitor, a duck called Scaup, also bred for the first time in 2001. Rumours even abound within Irish birding circles that Snowy Owls are now breeding somewhere in the country … a wonderful addition if it's true.

So what of the future? Climate change may be the most influential factor on future colonisations. If climate changes make for hotter summers, it's possible that southern breeding birds may arrive on our shores. Likely candidates could include Great White and Cattle Egrets, Black-winged Stilts or even Audouin's Gulls. These beautiful, large, red-billed gulls are beginning to move away from their western Mediterranean range and have regularly been seen in northern France. They have also been recorded in Britain in recent years. Hoopoes are even a possibility. These buff-pink birds with black-and-white wings and long crests are more often seen around Mediterranean holiday resorts. Yet each spring, more and more are

being seen in Ireland. Two birds even spent several weeks together at what seemed a perfect breeding spot. They didn't breed (perhaps it was two males or two females), but it could so easily have happened. Already, classic southern species such as the streaked Fan-tailed Warbler (or Zitting Cisticolas, as they are now known) are making their way northwards through France, while the rich brown Cetti's Warbler has conquered England and is working its way into Wales. One was heard singing along the Wicklow coastline in the summer of 2005 … the first coloniser?

It really is impossible to know, but without claiming to be a clairvoyant, I will don my fortune-teller's hat and suggest what species may arrive to breed in Ireland over the next ten years. I see Woodlarks in the forests of Wicklow and Ospreys on remote lakes of Donegal. I see myself sitting quietly on a summer's evening listening to the sweet, loud song of a Cetti's Warbler in Wexford. I can also hear the 'zitting' calls of Fan-tailed Warblers as they fly, in their bouncing fashion, over the marshy scrubland nearby. Perhaps this is fanciful dreaming on my part, but in 1981, such dreams were made of Little Egrets, Mediterranean Gulls, Reed Warblers and Great Skuas. Sometimes it's best not to ponder too much on where dreams end and reality begins!

PART 2

Chapter 15

Ten Steps to Bird Identification

Mistle Thrush *(Anthony McGeehan)*

Have you ever caught a quick glimpse of a bird and been left scratching your head, wondering what you've just seen? You have? Welcome to the 'hoodwink' gang. Frustrating, isn't it? What's even worse is when you've seen the bird very well, maybe even spent time examining it in great detail, and you still don't know what it is. It doesn't have to be like that, however. The skill of bird identification is not quantum physics. You don't need to be an Albert Einstein to be able to identify birds. True, some species can be more difficult to identify than others. Some even require very detailed and careful observation, but there are very few birds that you'll encounter in Ireland that can't be easily identified. It is time to let you into a little secret … there really is no such thing as a bird expert. Anyone can do it. In fact, in my opinion, bird identification is simply a process of elimination.

Let me give you an analogy. Imagine you're asked to enter a room of 300 people and given the task of finding your best friend among the crowd. It isn't really that hard, is it? A quick glance around the room and you find him/her. How did you do that? Well, you know this person very well. You can pick him/her out from the crowd without any difficulty. You didn't have to double-check to see if you were making a mistake because you know their identification features. It would be equally easy if you were asked to pick out members of your own family, your relatives or neighbours from among the crowd. It's the same with birds. Consider the birds you see in your garden as your friends, family and neighbours. You see them almost every day. You know them well and it isn't hard to pick them out from the crowd. You know their identification features.

One of the easiest of all birds to identify, a Kingfisher. If only they were all so easy *(Richard T. Mills)*

Let me take this analogy a little further. There are many people that you know well, even though you don't see them every day. Perhaps they are people you meet only when you go out at weekends. Perhaps they are people you only see when you go shopping. You recognise them instantly when you see them, even though you only meet them at these locations. Should you meet these people out of context, however, it might take a little time to figure out who they are because you are used to seeing them only at a specific location. These specific locations are like different habitats. When out birding, you'll find some birds only at specific habitats. You recognise them instantly within that habitat, but should you encounter a bird away from its normal habitat, it might take a little time to figure out what it is.

Anyone who has started a new job will know what it's like trying to remember everyone's name and what it is they do. On your first day, it can be a little overwhelming as you're introduced to lots of new faces and new tasks. Moments of panic set in as you wonder if you will ever remember them all. This is exactly like visiting a new habitat for the first time. There are new birds to learn, new calls to listen to and new identification challenges to face. It can be a little overwhelming at times. But after a week, it's surprising how many people (birds) you know. Visit this habitat on a regular basis for six months and you'll soon realise how many people (birds) you actually do know very well. In fact, you can instantly recognise a new face when you see one.

Let me return to this analogy one more time. Imagine you're now asked to enter the same room of 300 people, but they are all total strangers to you. Your task is to select one person from the crowd. You are given details of the person you are looking for. The main features are: she is a tall girl with long, brown hair and blue eyes. As you glance through the room, you immediately eliminate many people from the equation in seconds — all the men in the room, those with short hair, those with red or blonde hair etc. You may then be left with three girls roughly matching that description. On looking closer, only one of them has blue eyes … bingo! … you've found the person you're looking for.

You have succeeded in your task because, subconsciously, you have taken in a huge volume of detail and asked yourself many questions about all the

It looks like some kind of bunting, and it's near reeds. Could be a Reed Bunting? *(Tom Cuffe)*

A large thrush *could* be a Fieldfare, but not if you see it in summer *(Anthony McGeehan)*

118

people in the room. This all happens very quickly and your brain processes the information to give you a result. It is this subconscious process of elimination that I've tried to capture and break down into my 'Ten Steps' because, believe it or not, bird identification is exactly the same. Searching for a Chaffinch among the Greenfinches, a Little Stint among Dunlin, or a Mediterranean Gull among Black-headed Gulls is exactly the same as looking for a person in the crowd. Some are birds you know very well (your friends and family), others you don't know but you have the main identification features and you eliminate all those birds that don't match the features you expect to see. It can be difficult at first, but with experience it gets faster and easier.

The steps can be broken down into two sets. The first set are generic questions, looking at general information to hand, while the second set requires you to look a little closer at the bird and see key features that will lead to the identification.

Step One: What time of year is it?

This is a very important first question because many birds are present at different times of the year. There are summer migrants and winter visitors, as well as birds that pass through (or by) Ireland in spring and/or autumn. For example, a large thrush flying across the road in July will almost certainly be a Mistle Thrush; if it is winter, Fieldfare needs to be considered. In a harbour, a large diving bird that shows dark upperparts and white underparts may be a Great Northern Diver if it is winter, but will most probably be a young Cormorant if seen in July. The amount of other, similar examples is countless, but it's a vital first question and can quickly eliminate many possible confusion birds from the equation.

Step Two: Where is the bird?

This is another vital step in the process of elimination because many species prefer specific habitat types. Dunlin and Purple Sandpipers are two small, reasonably dull waders. Both have longish bills and both are usually found on the coast in winter. However, Dunlin usually feed on mudflats while Purple Sandpiper prefer seaweed-covered rocks and are rarely found on open, exposed estuaries (although Dunlin can also occur on rocky shores). Eider ducks are true sea ducks, while Mallard prefer freshwater

Knowing that Purple Sandpipers frequent seaweed-covered rocks can help identify them *(Anthony McGeehan)*

Although Buff-breasted Sandpiper (top) and Ruff look similar, the habitat can give a strong clue to the identity — Buff-breasts rarely wade into water while Ruffs feed along muddy channels and pools *(Top: Eric Dempsey. Bottom: Sean Cronin)*

Dippers are found on fast-flowing rivers and 'dip' under the water when feeding *(Anthony McGeehan)*

lakes and marshes. Even when birds appear to be in the same habitat, taking a closer look may reveal a lot. In autumn, both Ruff and Buff-breasted Sandpiper can occur in the same place, but Ruff feed along the muddy edges of pools while Buff-breasts rarely wade into water, preferring dry, open grassland. There are countless examples of how this works. In short, the habitat in which a bird is found can give very important clues as to its identity.

Step Three: What is the bird doing?

A bird's behaviour can be one of the most vital elimination factors in this process. Imagine a large, freshwater lake full of duck in winter (the first two steps covered), but how do we identify them? Such ducks can be broken into two categories: diving and surface-feeding species. There are several ducks that appear to have reddish heads and grey backs — are they Wigeon or Pochard? If they are diving, they are most certainly Pochard; if they are feeding on the

grass on the bank shore or dabbling on the surface, they're Wigeon. Even on nut-feeders in winter, different bird behaviour is easy to observe. Have you ever noticed that Siskins tend to feed upside-down, whereas Greenfinches never do? It's so easy when you remember that some birds are even named according to their behaviour: wagtails wag their tails; Turnstones turn stones over; Kingfishers catch fish; Treecreepers creep up trees; Dippers dip under the water etc.

Step Four: What size is it?

This is a key question. Never mind trying to put actual measurements to the bird. Instead, compare it with a familiar and, if possible, a similar-looking bird. For example: it is bigger than a Robin, but smaller than a Blackbird; it is bigger than a Dunlin, but smaller than a Redshank; it's about the size of a Magpie, but with a shorter tail. Using such techniques to judge the size of an unfamiliar species will always give a more accurate impression of size.

Step Five: What isn't it?

This is one of the most important questions of all because I believe that half the battle in bird identification is in knowing what the bird is not. This is based on the fact that no matter how new you are to birding, you'll have a wealth of information already stored and ready for use. Again, imagine a garden nut-feeder in winter. You know the usual birds that you see, so when a small, strange 'green' finch turns up, you're puzzled. Nonetheless, straightaway you know it isn't a Greenfinch. This vital piece of the elimination process can lead you on to your identification. What other Greenfinch-like bird can turn up … a Siskin? Let's check some details: it's definitely smaller than a Greenfinch; while it's also on the nut-feeder, it's actually feeding upside-down; and … it's wintertime. This step is vital every time you go out birding, whether you're looking at waders, gulls, ducks or warblers. Remember, use the familiar species as the starting-point and work from there.

Now it's time to begin observing details on the bird itself. This can be confusing at first, but the following steps will make it a little easier.

Step Six: What is the first thing that strikes you about the bird?

This can be anything at all. Is it tall, short, fat and dumpy? Does it have an evil eye or a gentle eye? Is it extraordinarily tame? Does it have bright red legs, a long bill, a short bill? It might even remind you of your Aunt Mary! For example, to my eye the posture of Starlings gives the impression that they have their 'hands in their pockets'. This is known as the 'jizz' of a bird. The word jizz is supposedly derived from the words 'general impression of size and shape', but has been abbreviated to jizz. The jizz of a bird is its personality. It captures how the bird behaves, moves, stands and looks. It's at this point that I must mention how important I believe note-taking is. You can read volumes about bird identification, but nothing else

Oystercatchers are very striking in flight *(Sean Cronin)*

122

compares to your own observations or your impressions of a bird's jizz. Taking simple notes not only forces you to observe more; it also clarifies in your mind the key features that you're seeing when looking at the bird. Such notes also act as important references for the future. So, whatever the first thing that strikes you about the bird is, take note of it because chances are this first thing may be the identification clincher.

Step Seven: What is the first feature you notice on the bird?

While this is very similar to Step Six (and in many cases may have the same answer), it asks you to select the key feature you notice on the bird. It could be anything from the bright colour on the breast to the leg colour, from the white wingbars to the short bill. Whatever feature immediately grabs you, note it down. This is often the feature that identifies the bird. For example, I recently spoke to a person who saw

'birds with long crests on their head' feeding in his garden … Waxings? Some more clues: it was January; they were devouring berries off his Rowan trees; they were about the size and shape of Starlings (but they certainly weren't Starlings); and the most amazing thing about them (besides the crest) was how tame they were. No further plumage details required, your Honour … the jury is directed to submit a verdict of Waxwing! So always take note of that first feature. It can be the vital clue.

Step Eight: What other plumage features can you see?

Now it's time to examine the bird in detail. To do this properly, it's very useful to know the main plumage parts of a bird. Look at the diagram on page 124, which details the terms used to describe the plumage of a bird. It may be difficult to remember all the pieces at first, but with a little practice, it becomes easier.

The chestnut crown and black spot on the cheek of the Tree Sparrow (left) are key features that distinguish it from House Sparrow (right) *(Left: John Gallagher. Right: Joe Curtis)*

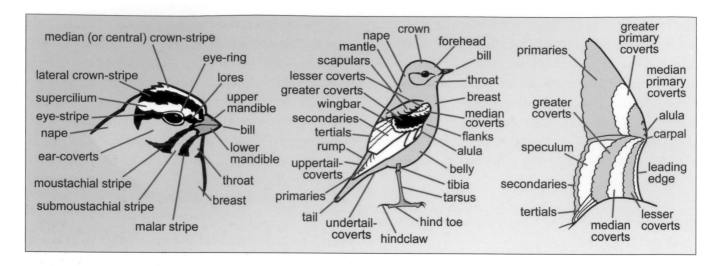

Practise trying to pick out the main plumage parts on common birds … you'll soon find that it's not as difficult as it first appears.

Try to note the following things, if possible:

• The face pattern — does the bird have a supercilium, a streaked crown, a moustachial stripe or an eye-ring?

• The upperparts — what is the main colour; is there streaking or barring?

• The wings — made up of main flight feathers and smaller, less important feathers that cover them (the coverts). Check for wingbars (which are formed by the tips to the coverts). Do the wings appear long? What colours are you seeing?

• The underparts — again, the main colours, are they streaked or barred; do the colours change from the breast onto the belly; is the streaking confined to the flanks only?

• The rump and tail — is the rump a different colour? Is the tail long, short, does it have white outer feathers?

• The bill — what is the shape, the length? Is it pointed or conical?

• The legs — are they long, short and what colour are they?

Step Nine: What is the call/song like?

Another very important thing to note is that many species are named after their song and call (Cuckoo, Chiffchaff and Kittiwake, to mention but a very few). Try to remember key phrases of the song. What was the

Waxwing — their long crests make them very distinctive
(Anthony McGeehan)

Skylark — another bird with a distinctive crest
(Anthony McGeehan)

rhythm of the song? Try to note whether the call had an upward or a downward inflection. Was it sharp, explosive, soft, or did the bird even call at all? Was the song delivered deep in cover, or out on the top of a tree? Was it singing as it flew in the air, like a Skylark? Did the bird call in flight or, like Long-tailed Tits, when it was feeding in a group? Looking at many books, it can be impossible to interpret others birders' transcriptions of bird songs and calls. Everyone's hearing is slightly different, so try to note your own version of what you hear. Even put your own words to the song. I recently heard some of the phrases of a Mistle Thrush song described as 'over here birdy'! When I later listened to the song myself, I too was able to hear those words. Another well-known example is the song of the Yellowhammer, which is traditionally transcribed as 'a

It's black and white, and wags its tail — Pied Wagtail
(*John Finn*)

The clue can be in the name, and in the song — Cuckoo
(*Anthony McGeehan*)

Kittiwakes calling (*Adrian Dancy*)

little bit of bread and no cheese'. I have to admit, I can hear the 'cheese' bit at the end of this song, but I really do think that the person who described the first section as a 'little bit of bread' was on drugs!

Step Ten: What is the flight like?
Last, but by no means least, is the bird's flight. The way a bird flies can often lead to the identification.

A hovering Kestrel *(Paul Kelly)*

Snipes when flushed will rise rapidly, call and fly off in a zig-zag pattern before landing a good distance away. The very similar Jack Snipe, on the other hand, will rise a little slower, fly silently in a very straight line and land a short distance away. Other things to check for are whether the wing flaps are fast like a wader or slow and laboured like a heron's. Are the wings long and pointed like a falcon, or broad and rounded like a Buzzard? Does the bird glide over the waves like a shearwater (hence their name), or flutter over the sea like a petrel? Does it hover like a Kestrel? Do the wings have wingbars, or do they appear plain and unmarked?

So, that's it … easy, isn't it? It may take a little time, but by using some or all of these steps combined, most birds can be identified easily. Remember, so-called bird experts are simply people who have a wider circle of 'bird' friends than you. It can sometimes take hard work to develop and maintain long-lasting friendships, but it's worth the effort. A world without friends is a very lonely place indeed.

Yellowhammer — a little bit of bread and no cheese! *(Sean Cronin)*

Chapter 16

Birding Begins at Home
— Winter Garden Birds

Long-tailed Tit *(John Finn)*

I just love the winter, don't you? Those cold, wet, windy days when you'd hardly be tempted to stick your nose outside the door are the very ones that afford me some of the best birding in my favourite habitat — my own back garden. Perhaps that's why I like winter so much. Yes, you can keep the North Bull Island and its thousands of waders and ducks; the North Slob in Wexford with half the world's population of Greenland White-fronted Geese might be an impressive sight to some, but you just can't beat your own garden in winter.

Living on the north side of Dublin, I am very lucky to have places like Glasnevin Cemetery and the National Botanical Gardens (or 'The Bots', as it's known locally) right beside me. These form an undisturbed green oasis in an urban setting, while the old ditches that once formed ancient borders to the fields upon which our houses are built have been left intact. It's such a shame that modern housing developments no longer keep these ancient ditches as natural boundaries to estates. As a result of far-sighted developers, those living in my area have mature Oak, Elderberry and Whitethorn trees forming mini-avian highways along our back gardens. Those living in more rural settings have thousands of kilometres of hedgerows and trees criss-crossing the land like an enormous 'spaghetti junction'.

With birds commuting along these highways throughout the day, it's easy to encourage them to take a detour and visit your garden. The enticement, of course, is food, and perhaps the easiest way to attract birds quickly into a garden is to hang up some nut-feeders and seed-feeders. These are fantastic inventions, coming in all shapes and sizes, and by simply moving them closer to the window each day,

Goldfinch — a recent visitor to nut-feeders *(Michael Finn)*

127

the birds become so tame that they hardly fly when you go out to refill the feeders. My feeders provide hours of entertainment as Greenfinches and Blue, Great and Coal Tits feed in dizzying rotation. In recent years, Goldfinches have learned to feed from them, too, and they certainly make a colourful addition to the garden list. House Sparrows have also learned to use the feeders, but because of their drab colours are not often as appreciated as their more flamboyant cousins. They are all welcome to my garden. To my astonishment, I have recently seen Goldcrests on my nut-feeders, and Reed Buntings have started to come to seed-feeders in some parts of the country. It seems the word is out in the world of birds … garden feeders are all the rage.

Having a well-stocked bird table brings in another collection of species, with Robins, Dunnocks, Chaffinches and Blackbirds all congregating each morning. Add a little coarse grain and you may attract Collared Doves. These elegant doves originated in Asia, but spread across Europe during the 20th century. In 1959, this species bred for the first time in Ireland, with the first pair being found close to Glasnevin Cemetery. Perhaps the ancestors of these first Irish colonists are now visiting my garden. In addition to the feeders and the bird table, creating a bird-friendly garden by planting shrubs like *Pyracantha* and *Cotoneaster* bushes or trees like Mountain Ash is worth considering. By September, they are laden with berries, ready for the winter-feeding, while the evergreen shrubs provide shelter and cover. These factors alone will draw in an appreciative audience of birds each year.

Birds struggle in winter and species employ a wide range of different approaches in order to survive. In autumn, many go through a complete moult, giving them new (and sometimes more) feathers to combat the cold, while extra fat put on in late autumn means many birds can weigh as much as one-third more in winter than they do in summer. In order to maintain this weight during the winter, small birds may need to eat as much as one-quarter their body weight each day to survive and therefore will spend from dawn to dusk searching for food. Water is also essential, particularly during cold snaps when, as well as needing to drink, birds need to wash and preen to keep those all important insulating feathers in perfect condition. Last, but not least, birds also need shelter in bad weather and for that reason, many species form large winter roosts. Starlings can form some spectacular

A Blue Tit enjoys peanuts, one of the most popular foodstuffs in winter (*Annette Cutts*)

A Great Tit feeding on suet balls, a mix of fat, nuts, seeds and breadcrumbs (*Adrian Dancy*)

A Coal Tit feeding from a bag of sunflower seeds. They will often hide or bury them for later (*John Finn*)

A female Greenfinch cracking barley seeds with her strong bill *(Annette Cutts)*

A male Blackbird *(Adrian Dancy)*

Chaffinches are one of the commonest garden birds in Ireland *(Michael Finn)*

roosts involving thousands of birds and are a familiar sight on a winter evening in towns and cities as they gather on aerials to spend the night, packed closely together for warmth. Pied Wagtails can also take advantage of the warmer city temperatures and hundreds of birds used to be seen in O'Connell Street, in Dublin, sleeping up against the Christmas lights in December. Alas, the felling of the mature trees in the street has resulted in this traditional roosting flock being widely dispersed across the city. The sight of so many wagtails together is now a memory of the past for Dubliners.

Providing food on a constant basis sustains many birds through some hard times, but it's vital to note that once you start, you should not stop as birds become dependent on your garden as an important food source. It always amazes me how quickly birds find out that you've starting feeding again each autumn. Once one bird discovers your garden, others soon follow. It seems like they have an avian grapevine working … 'Psst, did you hear that Dempsey has just filled those feeders again? Pass it on.'

With all this bird activity outside your window, it's easy to get a little blasé about the species you're seeing, but have you ever wondered where all those birds actually come from? While most of the species we find in our gardens in winter are common in Ireland all year round, it would be very unusual to see ten or 15 Blackbirds feeding together in one place during the summer months. Yet on cold winter days, that's exactly what you might see. For that matter, I've

Ringing studies show that dozens of Blue Tits can visit a particular garden each day in winter *(Annette Cutts)*

never seen more than a few pairs of Mistle Thrushes in Glasnevin during the breeding season, and yet in December it's not unusual to see hundreds flying overhead, giving their distinctive rattling calls.

Looking at the nut-feeders, you could also be forgiven for thinking that you have a resident group of five or six Blue Tits spending the whole day in your garden … but think again. Ringing studies have shown that perhaps as many as 100 Blue Tits can visit a garden in one day. So where are they all coming from?

In winter, Irish birds perform mini-migrations, with many species engaging in altitudinal migration (they leave the higher, colder areas to winter on the lowlands or along the coast). If the weather turns cold, many woodland species move out of their usual habitats in search of food and find their way into gardens, attracted by the regular food supply. In other species, females — weighing less than males and therefore less capable of storing enough fat reserves to see them through a hard winter — fly south to France, leaving a 'male-only' population behind to defend the territory (typical!). This explains why you usually just see one Robin in your garden in winter. The male Robin stays behind while the female migrates. This also explains why the Robin is one of the few birds that sings throughout the winter … he needs to sing in order to defend a territory.

Weather has the biggest influence on our winter birds. Remember that Ireland lies on the western edge of Europe, and as a result, our climate is dominated by the mild Atlantic weather systems. Because of this, we

Male Robins remain on their territory all year (*Joe Curtis*)

A House Sparrow enjoys a bath — a place to drink and bathe is very important for birds in winter *(John Fox)*

Redwing feeding on berries *(Denise Bowden)*

rarely suffer the harsh winter weather that grips our European neighbours each year. As winter takes hold in Europe, birds begin to move westwards in an attempt to avoid the bad weather and to find food. Each winter, Blackbirds, Mistle Thrushes, Redwings and Fieldfares migrate to Ireland in their hundreds of thousands, with equally large numbers of finches on the move as well, including Chaffinches, Siskins and Redpolls. These finch flocks can merge and form large, mixed groups that often include the classic winter finch, the boldly coloured Brambling.

Even the Starlings we have in our gardens in winter may well be birds that were hatched in the suburbs of a Scandinavian town or city last summer. More surprising is the fact that species like Coal Tits are also long-distance winter migrants from Northern Europe and Britain. European Coal Tits are easily identified by their clean, grey upperparts and pure white cheeks and nape patch. British birds appear very

similar, but they never look quite as clean or crisp as the European birds. By comparison, Irish birds appear quite yellowish on the head and show buffish-toned upperparts.

In recent years, apples placed strategically around the garden provide winter-feeding for Blackcaps. This robust, attractive warbler is now common in winter. The male shows a dusky grey plumage with a jet black cap, while the browner females display a rich chestnut crown. As discussed in Chapter 10, 'Permission to Land?', it is believed that Ireland's wintering population of Blackcaps come from Central Europe. Regardless of their origins, they add a certain touch of class to an Irish garden. In recent winters, Lesser Whitethroats (scarce autumn vagrants that are related to Blackcaps) were found wintering in suburban gardens, the first such winter records for this species. Will they, too, become as regular a sight in our gardens in winter as the Blackcap has?

Waxwings appear in large numbers in some winters, but may be absent in others *(Joe Curtis)*

If there is a very hard spell of cold weather in Europe, birds begin to flood into Ireland. During such conditions, the Irish night sky becomes alive with the calls of migrating birds. The easiest to identify are the soft, high-pitched calls of Redwings. In the garden, feisty, foreign Redpolls and Siskins join your familiar nut-feeding species, while your Blackcaps are competing with hosts of Scandinavian Blackbirds, Redwings and Fieldfares for their share of the apples. Thankfully, there is enough food to go around and because of our relatively mild climate, both our visitors and our resident species enjoy a lower winter mortality rate than those that stay on continental Europe. Once they are here, the birds tend to stay put, regardless of any improvements in the weather, leaving some areas of Europe virtually empty of songbirds.

Occasionally Ireland experiences the arrival of so-called 'irruptive' species. The most exotic of these is undoubtedly the colourful Waxwing, named because of the red waxy tips to the adult secondary feathers. They breed in northern Europe and occasionally experience a drastic food shortage in their usual wintering areas in Europe. When this happens, they form large roving flocks, moving westward in search of berries — their staple food in winter. When they occur, these dramatic movements are known as 'irruptions'. Waxwings are wonderfully tame birds and extremely vocal; their trilling calls sound like modern telephones ringing. In some winters, Waxwings arrive in such large numbers that single flocks can contain as many as 500 birds. During such irruptions, it is easy to get an impression that Waxwings can be found wherever there are berries to be eaten.

With birds moving in such numbers during winter, it is possible for any species to turn up. As gardens seem to be the most watched habitats in winter, and as any rare or unusual bird will probably be moving with common birds, there is every likelihood that something very special will turn up in your garden. I've watched a couple of Great Spotted Woodpeckers coming to nut-feeders in gardens, while one lucky person in Swords, in Dublin, played host to Ireland's second ever Pine Bunting, a rare Siberian species. It fed alongside the sparrows, finches and Yellowhammers, totally oblivious to the fuss it had caused. I also know of two people who have even seen a Hawfinch feeding with the Greenfinches on their feeders.

The best I have seen in my own garden is a group of 35 Waxwings and a wintering Chiffchaff, but I know anything is possible. Even North American species that may have found their way across the Atlantic in the autumn have been found in gardens. Spending the winter in Ireland, they, like our resident species, are struggling to survive and become dependent on a regular food supply if it's available. For example, the majority of Irish records of American Robins — large colourful, Blackbird-sized thrushes — refer to birds feeding in gardens in winter. Likewise, in Europe the majority of reports of a Siberian species called Black-throated Thrush have been in people's gardens. This species has yet to be recorded in Ireland, but I'm positive that the first sighting will be in someone's garden, feeding on apples or berries along with the Blackbirds … hold on, what was that on the apples?

High on every birder's Garden Wish List, an American Robin. Some day ... *(Matt Latham)*

Chapter 17

Awash with Seabirds

Razorbill *(Clive Timmons)*

The rugged Irish coastline, with its rocky shores, remote islands, sea-stacks and cliffs, has been shaped by the power of the sea over tens of thousands of years. Surrounded by food-rich waters, this habitat is ideal for breeding seabirds, and few European countries can surpass the variety and sheer numbers found along our coastline.

In summer, sea cliffs can provide some of the most exciting birding, with thousands of birds

Guillemots packed onto a cliff ledge *(Eric Dempsey)*

crammed onto the narrowest of ledges on the steepest stretches in 'high-rise' fashion. Among them are two members of the auk family, the Razorbill and the Guillemot. Both are black above and white below and are best told apart by the shape of their bills. Guillemots have long, pointed bills, while those of Razorbills are thicker and blunter with distinctive white markings. Alongside them are the only true Irish breeding 'sea gull', the Kittiwake. These birds have yellow-green bills with a white head and white underparts, while their pearl-grey upperparts are completed by neat black wingtips. Unlike many other gulls found along the coast, they have dark eyes, which gives them a gentler expression. Kittiwakes build small, cup-shaped nests from seaweed and other materials; Guillemots and Razorbills don't bother with nests at all. These birds are so adapted to nesting on sheer cliffs that their eggs are cone-shaped, so that if an adult should disturb it, it will roll in on itself in a complete circle rather than off the cliff face.

Shags and their larger cousins, Cormorants, can be found on the wider ledges, while Fulmars seem to prefer the highest areas on the cliffs. Fulmars initially appear gull-like, but are in fact a member of the petrel and shearwater family. All of these birds are known as 'tubenoses' because they have external nostrils (unlike most other birds, which simply have a slit in their bills). These 'tubenoses' give these birds a good sense of smell (vital if searching for food in the open

Fulmar *(Michael Finn)*

Gannets *(Joe Curtis)*

oceans), as well as helping to secrete excess salt from their bodies. On quieter, more gently sloping cliffs on undisturbed headlands and islands, our most charming and colourful seabird is found: the Puffin. Nesting in disused burrows, adult Puffins can be seen at this time of year returning with sand eels draped carefully in their extraordinary bills.

Gannets, our largest seabird, are currently enjoying an expansion of their breeding areas. Up until recently, Gannets only nested on the Bull Rock in Cork, on Clare Island in Mayo, on the Great Saltee Island in Wexford and on the Skelligs in Co. Kerry, where over 25,000 pairs form one of the largest colonies in Europe. Such has been their breeding success in recent years that a second colony has emerged on the stacks off the Saltees, while on the narrow stack behind Ireland's Eye in Dublin, a few pairs began nesting in the early 1990s. In more recent years, the Dublin colony has grown considerably and it seems that there is hardly any space left on the stack … time to look elsewhere, perhaps? Gannets take several years before reaching maturity. Moulting each year, the birds gradually change from their brownish,

immature plumage before eventually being transformed into the pristine white, black-wing-tipped and yellow-headed plumage of adults. Gannets have binocular vision and dive from great heights into the sea in pursuit of their quarry. With swept-back wings, they hit the water at great speed, but have 'avian air-bags' in their skulls that absorb the impact of such dives. With so many gulls waiting on the water to snatch an easy meal, Gannets will usually have swallowed their catch before they surface again.

Young birds everywhere have voracious appetites, and seabird chicks are no different. The activity, noise and smell of a seabird colony are undoubtedly an experience not to be missed. But perhaps one of the most surreal summer experiences can be found on the remotest islands when Manx Shearwaters and Storm Petrels land under the cover of dark, moonless nights. Being almost helpless on the ground, it's safer for them to return on dark nights, as otherwise they would be easy prey for gulls and other predators. Their eerie calls echo around the islands as thousands of birds return to feed their hungry chicks. Nesting in burrows, Manx Shearwaters are the commonest of the shearwater family found in Irish waters. These black-and-white birds are like mini-albatrosses, flying vast distances using the updrafts

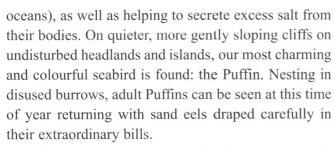

Shag *(John Fox)*

created by the waves. Gliding and banking effortlessly, their wingtips almost shear the water (hence the name) as they adjust to the slightest change in the air speed or direction.

Storm Petrels, of which Ireland has the world's largest breeding population, concentrated on the islands off Co. Kerry, are even more remarkable. Nesting in wall crevices or under rocks, these birds spend over ten months each year at sea. In flight, they almost look like Swifts, having an all-black plumage and a small white rump. It's truly extraordinary to see these tiny, sparrow-sized birds flutter and glide just above the waves, dropping down into the water to feed on small fish and plankton, totally unconcerned by the turbulent waters around them. Ireland also has a very

small breeding population of the slightly larger and similarly plumaged Leach's Petrels. These birds have nested on the extremely remote Stags of Broadhaven in Mayo, although they may be present on other windswept and inaccessible Irish islands in the Atlantic.

The hustle and bustle of these colonies continues into late summer until, almost as if a magic spell has been cast, the cliffs and islands fall silent. Thousands of birds leave the breeding sites and move far out to sea. Streaming down to join them are countless thousands more, which have bred on similar sites in Scotland and northern Europe. While many species spend the winter in the North Atlantic, many more are beginning their southward migration, and the months

A Storm Petrel, close to its nesting burrow on a small island off Kerry *(Michael O'Clery)*

138

of August and September are perhaps the best times for what birders know as seawatching.

Seawatchers are a special breed of birder, willing to spend hours from dawn until dusk watching the movements of seabirds. Of course, most of the migration takes place far out to sea, so the best seawatching is done when storm-force winds and rain force the birds closer to shore. Throughout August and September, headlands like Ramore Head in Antrim, Kilcummin in Mayo, the Bridges of Ross in Clare, and the headlands and islands off the south-western counties of Kerry and Cork attract these hardened birders in the most atrocious weather conditions. Sitting precariously on the most open headlands and island tips, seawatchers examine in detail the lines of birds moving before them. It's a skill in itself to pick out, for example, a single Leach's Petrel among thousands of Storm Petrels, but the greatest skill is in explaining where it is to others as they gaze out onto an open sea.

Among the most obvious of the birds moving south are the pirates of the sea, the skuas. The largest of these gull-like birds is the Great Skua (or Bonxies, to give them their Scottish Isles' name). They are buff-brown with white wing patches. These aggressive birds harry and chase other seabirds to force them to regurgitate their food, usually catching and eating the regurgitated food before it hits the water. Pomarine and Arctic Skuas also pass through Irish waters each autumn and look very alike. Arctics are smaller and

Great Skua — pirate of the High Seas *(Anthony McGeehan)*

Adult Pomarine Skua *(Anthony McGeehan)*

Adult Long-tailed Skua *(Anthony McGeehan)*

appear more lightweight than their larger, barrel-chested cousins. Adult Arctic Skuas also show two pointed tail feathers, while the tails of Pomarine Skuas show twisted, 'spoon-shaped' central feathers. Both species have 'light' and 'dark' phases, with light phase birds being dark above and white below, and dark phase birds, as their name suggests, showing an all-dark plumage. Like Bonxies, they also show white wing flashes and both also employ the rather unsavoury feeding tactic of chasing birds until they regurgitate their food.

One of the greatest spectacles is an aerial battle between skuas and the highly manoeuvrable terns and Kittiwakes. The skuas usually win out in the end. Until recently, the smallest, most elegant and least aggressive of the skuas, the Long-tailed Skua, was considered to be very rare in Irish waters. However, a better understanding of the weather patterns that may affect the migration of these birds has allowed birders to predict when they may occur, while advances in their identification make them easier to recognise. An interesting development is the recent breeding of Great Skuas in Ireland. Birds have nested on the

remote islands off Mayo and look set to become a settled Irish breeding species … although I don't think the local seabirds will welcome the new neighbours from hell!

An understanding of the weather is vital to predict where to go for the best seawatching. It's pointless to sit on Kilcummin Head with a southerly wind, for example. Areas like that produce the best birds in strong north-westerlies, when birds are forced into the large bays of north Mayo and battle against the wind, hugging the coastline as they make their way back out into the Atlantic. Likewise, Cape Clear Island in Cork is best in strong south-westerly winds, when birds are blown onto the southern Irish coastline.

The 'large shearwaters' are among the most sought-after birds, and a Cory's Shearwater gliding on bowed wings in Irish waters is a sight to behold. These pale brown and white shearwaters fly in a slow,

A Wilson's Petrel — the 'Holy Grail' for many Irish birders
(Anthony McGeehan)

Seawatchers at the Bridges of Ross in Clare *(Victor Caschera)*

unhurried 'mañana-like' manner that is typical of their Mediterranean origins. By contrast, the Great Shearwater is more striking both in plumage (it has a black cap) and in its more direct, hurried style of flight. Both Great Shearwater and the all-dark Sooty Shearwater breed in the southern oceans but spend the southern winter north of the equator. Their migration takes them on a giant loop, first passing the eastern US coast before heading into the Labrador Banks off south-eastern Newfoundland, in Canada. This region consists of several large underwater banks that rise from the Continental Shelf. The cold Labrador Current, originating from the Arctic Ocean, crosses the banks and meets the warm Gulf Stream that flows along the eastern part of the region. The mingling of these two currents, combined with the shallowness of the water, provides a perfect environment for plankton, upon which fish depend for food. Naturally, seabirds thrive in this food-rich area. It makes an ideal stopover for the shearwaters before they continue their

loop south, this time off the European side of the Atlantic. Both species are usually found off Ireland every August and September, with Sooties occasionally matching (or even outnumbering) Manx Shearwaters off some areas, given ideal weather conditions.

As if clambering out onto the remotest headland tips in foul weather wasn't bad enough, Irish birders are now pushing their tolerance even further. In the mid-1980s, several birders hired boats and travelled far out towards the Continental Shelf in search of seabirds. They came back with tales of Sabine's Gulls, a petite North American species, and they saw Great Shearwaters and Grey Phalaropes feeding so close that they could almost touch them. Best of all, they also saw the much sought-after Wilson's Petrel. These are like Storm Petrels, with long, 'paddle-shaped' wings and long legs that extend beyond their tail. When feeding, they drop their feet into the water and perform a trampoline-like dance, almost as if they

Trawlers act like magnets to feeding seabirds *(Anthony McGeehan)*

were bouncing off the surface of the water. Breeding in the southern hemisphere, Wilson's Petrels winter in the western Atlantic but are rarely encountered on this side of the ocean. And so a new era in seabird watching dawned and 'the pelagic' was born.

Pelagics are now annual August events and involve travelling out to sea early in the morning and spending hours among the migrating seabirds. When birders come across a feeding flock, the engines are cut and the boat drifts with the current. If you're already feeling a little seasick at the thought of this, then prepare yourself for the worst. In order to attract seabirds, most birders arrange for several barrels of chum to be on board. Chum is a disgusting mixture of fish offal, fish oil and, if possible, old cooking oil. This mixture is left sealed in barrels for as long as possible so that it really stinks when opened. This horrible concoction is then gradually dished overboard, and it acts like a magnet for seabirds. While not always the most enjoyable type of birding,

pelagics can produce exciting results. Perhaps one of the most memorable birding moments for me occurred 3 km off Cape Clear, in Cork, in 1995, when a Black-browed Albatross buzzed our boat only 20 m from us. While the views of birds are superb on these trips, it is equally miraculous to see how quickly a person who only minutes before appeared close to death's door from seasickness can suddenly spring to life when an albatross flies by!

There is still much to discover about seabirds off Ireland. Each year, more and more sightings of unusual species are reported and any seabird species can conceivably pass the Irish coastline. In recent years, Fea's Petrels, a large grey and white petrel with dark underwings, have been seen annually. Breeding on the Cape Verde Islands and Madeira, this species was virtually unknown in Irish waters before the 1990s. Is there a difference in the feeding patterns of this species due to climate changes forcing the birds to travel further north than before? Or is it simply that

Sabine's Gull *(Anthony McGeehan)*

Great Shearwater *(Derek Charles)*

Fea's Petrel *(Paul Kelly)*

Leach's Petrel *(Anthony McGeehan)*

birders have become sharper observers and are seeing species that have been there all the time? It is impossible to answer, but I suspect somehow that seawatchers in the 1960s, 1970s and 1980s would have seen species like Fea's Petrels if they were there.

The presence or otherwise of seabirds is a sure indicator of the health of our waters. To know that our breeding colonies are thriving should comfort us. It really is worth taking the time to visit a seabird colony in summer. See, hear and smell for yourself the wonderful sights, sounds and aromas of a busy seabird colony. Or, if you're feeling a little more adventurous, settle down in August and September on a headland when there is a good onshore wind and enjoy an opportunity to witness some of the best seabird movements off any coastline in Europe. Seawatching can be hard sometimes, requiring a combination of skill and patience, but the rewards are rich for those willing to put in the time. Thankfully, for those 'landlubbers' among us, it now seems that even the elusive Wilson's Petrel can be seen from headlands, with more records seen from land than from pelagics in the last few years ... so keep watching and always expect the unexpected!

Chapter 18

A Walk on the Wild Side
— Ireland's Ducks

Wigeon *(Michael Finn)*

When I was young, I received a very unusual Christmas present. My name was registered with the British Wildfowl Trust's 'adopt a duck scheme'. This was a novel way for the Trust to gain much-needed funding to support their research work. For my present, a duck was caught and ringed in my name. The theory behind the scheme was that as 'an adopter', I would be kept up to date on any subsequent information they received on that specific bird. I had great visions of some exotic duck species being ringed on my behalf, so it was with great expectations and excitement that I opened the letter that duly arrived from Bristol with all the details. You can imagine my disappointment when I read those details … they had ringed a common old Mallard. Let's face it, the furthest this bird was going to fly was from the canal to the local duck pond in search of food. Exotic species indeed!

Time passed and I thought no more of my Mallard. Then several years later, and out of the blue, I was surprised when a card from the Wildfowl Trust plopped through the letterbox. It told of a great tragedy: my Mallard had been shot. Despite the obvious sense of sadness for any wild creature shot, my eyes were drawn to another line on the card … 'Location'. It was with utter astonishment that I read (and re-read) the information contained under that heading. It gave details of some unpronounceable lake in Central Siberia where 'my Mallard' had met its end.

Central Siberia? A Mallard, caught in Bristol ended up in Siberia? It was a revelation. Until then, I had always considered migrants to be birds like swallows, cuckoos and terns. True, I knew ducks arrived each winter, but it wasn't until that moment that I realised that they too were long-distance migrants, capable of making equally remarkable flights.

Ducks make great winter watching. They tend to swim on open water or feed on estuaries, and with over 30 species recorded in Ireland, there is enough of a variety to keep any birder entertained. Less than half of that number actually breed here, with some having extremely small breeding populations. For example, in Northern Ireland, as few as one or two pairs of Scaup have nested in recent years, while up to 5,000 birds can be found each winter on Lough Neagh alone. Likewise, Ireland holds fewer than 20 breeding pairs of Wigeon each summer. Yet by November, our coastal estuaries hold thousands. So most of the ducks we see in Ireland are purely winter visitors from northern and central Europe, from Iceland and Siberia. The one exception to the 'winter duck rule' is the Garganey. These are unique in being the only 'summer duck' visitor to Ireland, choosing to winter further south in Africa.

The other great thing that I like about ducks is that they are reasonably easy to identify (sighs of relief all around). Males (drakes) are invariably the more colourful as they don't require the camouflage at

A female Mallard showing the brightly coloured speculum on her wing *(Michael Finn)*

nesting time because few partake in the incubation or care of the young. Females (ducks) do most of the incubation and caring for the young, and as a result are usually the duller of the two. Drakes are also as bright and colourful in winter as in summer because most display and pair-bond in winter. Only some, the Long-tailed Duck for example, show different plumage in winter. Being aquatic, ducks need to keep their feathers in perfect condition and they spend hours each day preening and repairing feathers to maintain their insulation. They also bathe frequently and spend long periods applying an oily substance to their feathers from a special gland near their tails. Without this, they would lose their waterproofing and we

would never have been able to coin the phrase, 'water off a duck's back'.

So, where to start? Ducks comprise two main groups: surface-feeders (or dabblers) and divers. Next consideration is habitat preference: some are found on estuaries and freshwater, others only on freshwater lakes and marshes, and then there are perhaps my favourites, true seaducks.

Our largest duck is the Shelduck, a colourful bird usually found on estuaries. Nesting in disused rabbit burrows, females do not depend on camouflage for safety and so, unlike other duck species, are as brightly coloured as the males. The best way to sex them is that males tend to be slightly bigger and show

Shelduck crèche *(Adrian Dancy)*

a larger 'knob' on the top of the bright red bill. This is known as a 'shield' and once gave the species its name: 'Shield-duck'. This has now been shortened to 'Shelduck'. They feed very much like an Avocet, scooping their bill from side to side in search of tiny invertebrates. They also make great parents and in summer, various families join together to form large crèches of 50 or more ducklings that are accompanied by just two or three adults (I wonder how the decision is reached on who stays and who goes). This behaviour is adopted by birds like flamingos and penguins and concentrates the young birds in one good feeding area. Perhaps there is also an advantage for those adults that are minding the crèche. Could it

be that their ducklings stay within the centre of this large crèche, reducing the risk of predation? While the 'aunts' guard the crèches, the remainder of the adults will depart to the shallow mud and sandbanks of the south-east corner of the North Sea to moult (their post-nuptial moult). Up to 90,000 Shelducks gather here each summer from all around north-western Europe. The reason why they go to such a location is because ducks moult all their flight feathers at one time. Other bird species tend to moult in stages over a longer period, which allows them to continue flying. So, in late summer, ducks are flightless for a couple of weeks and they need to find safe areas to feed and rest during this period. For that reason, many drakes become drab and dull like females in late summer as they enter into eclipse plumage, as this plumage phase is called. They need to remain as inconspicuous as they can because during this time, their only method of escaping a predator is to swim.

On the water or mudflats, dabblers are best recognised by their long, spatula-shaped bills. Dabblers include Mallard, Wigeon, Teal, Pintail, Gadwall and, perhaps the most obvious of all, the Shoveler. This bill shape is ideal for grazing on grass and water vegetation (dabbling ducks being primarily vegetarians). Dabblers also feed constantly and process their meals fairly quickly. The classic estuary birds include Wigeon, Pintail, Teal and Shoveler, while Mallards are found anywhere from estuaries,

inland lakes, rivers to the local park. On the other hand, Gadwall, a handsome grey duck, is always found in freshwater habitats. When you look closely at these males, you'll see that the greys of their plumage are actually formed by very narrow, fine barring that blends in to give them their colour. Such fine barring is called vermiculation (derived from the Latin word, 'vermis', meaning a worm).

While dabbler-males are all well marked, the brown females can appear very similar to one another. Check for the size of the bird to start with. The length and colour of the bill is a good indicator, while the head shape is also a useful feature. Wigeon, for example, tend to have a very steep forehead and a bluish-grey bill; Shoveler an enormous bill; Pintail a

Wigeon *(Annette Cutts)*

Teal *(Eric Dempsey)*

Pintail *(Eric Dempsey)*

Gadwall *(Annette Cutts)*

grey and black bill, a long slender neck and a slim body; while Teal have an all dark bill and are tiny by comparison to them all. Dabblers are also easily identified in flight as they each have colourful patches on the secondary flight feathers called speculums (one more word for that ever-growing list). The colour of the speculum, as well as the colour of the borders to it, is unique to each species. Some also have bright markings on the front of the wing that further aid identification. While identifying ducks in flight takes a little getting used to, the colour of the speculum can also be useful when looking at ducks on the water. For example, a Gadwall's speculum is very obvious as a white patch, even when the bird is swimming. Every year sees the arrival of some dabblers from North America, blown across the Atlantic on their migrations. Many of these are the North American equivalents of our species, hence we occasionally see Green-winged and Blue-winged Teals and American Wigeon.

By comparison, diving ducks tend to be smaller than most dabblers and have short, broad, speculum-less wings and shorter, broader bills. In many species, the males are black and white, with most preferring freshwater lakes. Our commonest diving duck is the Tufted Duck. Males have black upperparts, a black breast, white belly and a black head with a distinctive long tuft on the rear of the crown (in the world of birds, tufts are feathers that tend to hang down, while crests are feathers that stand more erect). Scaup also

Tufted Ducks *(Annette Cutts)*

Garganey *(Mark Wilson)*

Pochard *(Sean Cronin)*

Scaup *(Anthony McGeehan)*

show a black head and breast but have grey upperparts, while Goldeneyes show a white spot on the face, a black head, and have an intricate black-and-white striped plumage. In good light, those black heads can turn into iridescent greens, purples and blues.

Like the dabblers, female divers can be a little tricky, but head shape is the key. Female Tufted have a rounded crown, a short tuft on the head, and can show a narrow white patch around the base of the bill; female Scaup are very similar, but besides being bigger show a square-shaped head and more extensive white on the face. Female Goldeneyes show a very pointed crown and a tiny bill. The exception to the black-and-white rule is the Pochard, with males showing a very striking chestnut head, a black breast and grey upperparts. Like the dabblers, the greys of these males are once again formed by vermiculations. All these diving ducks feed on aquatic insects, invertebrates and small fish. Such a high protein diet means

that they spend less time feeding and enjoy long periods of resting and preening … ideal for birders. We also get some exotic divers in Ireland, including Ring-necked Duck and Lesser Scaup from North America, and the unusually named Ferruginous Duck from central and eastern Europe.

I can't leave the diving ducks without mentioning those among the 'sawbills'. These birds are typified by having long, thin bills with a serrated edge (hence the name) that are perfect for catching fish. The commonest sawbill is the Red-breasted Merganser, found on freshwater lakes, estuaries, harbours and the open sea. The long, wispy tufts are the key identification feature, regardless of the sex of the bird. These wisps are lacking on the similar but larger Goosander, which was once a great winter rarity in Ireland. In recent years, Goosanders have colonised the east, with pairs now established on many lakes and fast-flowing rivers in the mountains of Wicklow. As a result, they are seen more frequently (usually on freshwater lakes,

Goldeneye (Annette Cutts)

reservoirs and rivers, although they are occasionally seen on the open sea). Last of the sawbills is the small, but exotic, Smew. Males again are black and white, with the more commonly seen females being duller brown above with an orange-red head that gives them the nickname of 'redheads'. A bird of northern Europe, small numbers occur here each winter, especially in northern counties.

Finally, come the real toughies of the duck world — the seaducks. These include Eider, the all-black Common Scoter and Long-tailed Ducks. It's remarkable to watch these ducks swim on the sea even during the roughest weather, bobbing up on the crests of waves like corks. Feeding on crustaceans, molluscs and other small animal life, it's even more remarkable to watch them dive effortlessly in such seas. Female Eiders line their nests with down plucked from their breast. This down is harvested without harming either the nest or eggs. The down is used in quilts and jackets, and anyone who has felt the comfort and warmth of such items will surely agree that eiderdown provides incredible insulation against the cold, which is essential if these birds are to survive the toughest elements of the winter. Like Shelducks, female Eiders will often gather their ducklings into large crèches in summer. Eiders can form large wintering flocks that are occasionally graced by a rarer cousin, the King Eider. These are birds of the high Arctic and the males are truly spectacular, showing a large orange shield to an orange bill, pale blue heads and two black sails on their backs.

Likewise, Common Scoters form large flocks in winter and attract small numbers of Velvet Scoter to their ranks. These Scandinavian ducks are easily identified in flight when their large, white wing patches make them obvious among the Common Scoters. Another scoter is also attracted to these large flocks and this is the Surf Scoter, a species from North America. Males show large orange-yellow bills and white head patches, but it's their skill in the water that

Eider (Adrian Dancy)

151

Red-breasted Merganser *(Clive Timmons)*   Long-tailed Duck *(Paul Kelly)*

makes them highly entertaining to watch. As their name suggests, these birds like to swim and feed in the surf of waves and would put many surfers to shame as they expertly ride the biggest breakers. In fact, birders call them 'surfers'.

I would like to end with a slight word of caution. Ducks are widely kept in many bird collections and zoos. Many unusual duck sightings may refer to fugitives from such places. Does that mean that all unusual duck sightings should be considered guilty until proven innocent? It can be a difficult thing to judge. For example, in January of 2006, a male Baikal Teal was found in Belfast. A bird of eastern Asia, it arrived overnight with several hundred European Teal. In ordinary circumstances, the origins of such a bird would be instantly under suspicion. However, its arrival coincided with some of the harshest winter weather continental Europe had experienced for years. Such weather had forced many birds westwards, seeking milder conditions and food. Its provenance was further enhanced when news came of another Baikal Teal record. This bird, a female, was shot in Denmark around the same time and scientific analysis of this unfortunate duck revealed that she had indeed

originated from Asia. She was a truly wild Baikal Teal. If a wild female can make it to Denmark, then surely a male could make it to Ireland under similar weather conditions?

The trouble is that, while some birds do appear to have perfect provenance, it is not always as it seems. Some years ago, on a lonely lake in Kerry, a female Hooded Merganser was found. An extremely rare North American species, this bird had everything going for it. It was found in the south-west of Ireland in early winter … surely this was the real thing? Then she climbed out of the water and proudly revealed the coloured rings on her legs. Birders had travelled from far and near to see this bird, only to realise that she had made good her escape from a zoo. So not all exotics are what they seem. Then again, not all common old ducks are what they seem. To this day, I still look at each Mallard I encounter and wonder whether it will spend the summer on the local pond or in some far-off lake, thousands of kilometres from Ireland. Perhaps some are even distant descendants of my long dead, but certainly not forgotten, adopted Siberian Mallard.

Chapter 19

The Original 'Wild Geese'

Brent Goose *(Clive Timmons)*

I started the previous chapter on a Christmas theme, and once again I find myself thinking of the festive season when it comes to geese. I'm sure you've heard the old rhyme that goes, 'Christmas is coming and the goose is getting fat' … but have you ever wondered what species of goose is getting fat? The traditional 'farmyard' goose is, in fact, a domesticated

Greylag Goose *(Derek Charles)*

descendant of the Greylag Goose. Geese and ducks are collectively referred to as 'wildfowl', but unlike ducks, all geese are vegetarians (in fact, most graze like cattle). Greylag is the bulkiest of the nine species of goose that have ever occurred in Ireland. However, that wasn't the deciding factor in selecting this species for domestication. Greylag is also the most southern breeding species. Therefore young and moulting adults (which, like all wildfowl, lose the ability to fly for a short period when moulting) were easily caught on the European breeding grounds and domesticated.

All geese are winter visitors to Ireland, but feral (formerly domesticated but now wild) populations of Greylag, along with smaller numbers of Canada Geese, are now breeding here and are found all year round. Geese that visit Ireland can be divided into two quite distinct groups: the 'grey' (really greyish-brown) and the 'black and white'. It is the 'grey' group that can cause more confusion because, at first glance, they are similar in colour. The key to their identification lies in taking note of a few simple things, such as the size of the bird, the colour of the bill and legs, as well as the actual colour tones of the plumage. Things are sometimes a little more complicated than they first appear and I'm afraid grey geese are no exception. Different races occur that vary in bill colour and occasionally plumage features, but with just five species to concentrate on, these birds can be identified.

Within the 'grey' group are Greylag, White-fronted, Pink-footed, Bean and the very rare Lesser White-fronted Goose. Let's look at each one separately. Greylag Goose is the largest of the group and show thickset, brownish heads and necks with darker neck stripes. Their upperparts are a similar colour, but show pale fringes to the feathers, giving them a banded appearance. The underparts are pale greyish brown and, like all geese in the 'grey' group, the area under the tail (the ventral area) is white. The legs are a dull pink, with European birds showing a thick orange bill. The Siberian race appears paler overall and shows a pink bill. Caution should always be exercised when judging colour, as orange and pink can appear very alike according to light and weather conditions. When in flight, the front part of the wing (the forewing) appears very pale grey and contrasts with the innerwing. This forewing colour gives Greylag Geese their name.

White-fronted Geese are very like Greylag but appear much darker brown overall, lacking the pale fringes to the upperpart feathers and showing distinct black patches on the belly. The most distinctive feature is the broad white patch at the base of the bill, which extends up onto the forehead (known as a blaze). On young birds, this blaze is very much reduced, but it becomes more prominent as the birds mature. The race that occurs in Ireland is the Greenland White-fronted Goose and it shows an orange bill. This feature distinguishes them from their

Greenland White-fronted Goose (Martin Garner)

European cousins, which show a pink bill. Both races have orange legs. In flight, their wings show very little contrast, appearing wholly brown.

Every winter, half of the world's population of Greenland White-fronted Geese (usually over 12,000 birds) visit the Wexford Wildfowl Reserve, and each year birders scour the flocks in the hope of finding a Lesser White-fronted Goose. These very endangered Arctic European and Asian birds winter primarily in the Caspian Sea region and the only record in Ireland was an individual seen on the Wexford Reserve back in March 1969. They are very similar to White-fronted, but are considerably smaller, with a neater pink bill and showing a very conspicuous yellow ring around the eye (an orbital ring). The best feature is the extent of the white blaze, which continues well past the forehead and onto the crown. A conservation programme currently under way in the Netherlands is attempting to encourage young birds to migrate south-west with Barnacle Geese, where shooting pressures are reduced and suitable habitats can be found. These birds have colour rings on their legs, but none have found their way to Ireland as yet, but it can only be a matter of time.

The next two species, Pink-footed and Bean Goose, are so alike that until relatively recently, they were considered to be variations of the same species. The Pink-footed Goose is the smallest of the 'grey' geese and, as the name suggests, they have very bright, obviously pink legs as well as small, stubby,

Pink-footed Goose *(Derek Charles)*

dark bills with a pink band towards the tip. Breeding in Greenland and Iceland, small numbers reach Ireland each winter. To my eye, Pink-footed Goose is one of the most aesthetically pleasing of all geese, showing a small, dark 'Bourneville' chocolate-coloured head and short neck, contrasting with a sandy-coloured breast and underparts. The upperparts are equally striking, being a 'frosty' bluish-grey that dominates the whole of the wing when seen in flight.

The Bean Goose, on the other hand, is a much more complex bird altogether. There are two distinct races, the 'taiga' and the 'tundra', and some taxonomists have in fact reclassified these as two distinct species, Taiga Bean Goose and Tundra Bean Goose. Both are very rare in Ireland, but the one most often encountered here is the Taiga Bean Goose. They appear very similar to Pink-footed Goose, showing the dark head and neck contrasting with pale underparts. Their bill patterns are also very alike, but the Taiga Bean Goose has a varying amount of orange on the bill as well as orange legs. They are also bigger and longer necked than Pink-footed Goose and lack the 'frosted' bluish-grey upperparts. In fact, the upperparts are quite plain in comparison, and in flight the wings lack any real contrast with the body.

Tundra Bean Goose is a different-looking bird, with some being as large as Greylag Goose. They too share the distinct features of Pink-footed and Taiga Bean Geese by having a dark head and neck that contrasts with paler underparts, while structurally they appear taller with long, thin necks. The bill shows an orange band just before the tip, similar in pattern to that of Pink-footed Goose. The legs are also orange. When they are found, they are often with Greylag Geese and can sometimes be difficult to pick out among them. In flight, however, their wings appear quite plain and they can be easily seen among a flock of Greylags.

When lone birds are found, it can often be difficult to tell one race from the other and it seems that the key feature to look for is the shape of the bill. The bill of Taiga Bean is usually quite long and slender towards the tip, while that of Tundra tends to be shorter, blunter and quite thick at the base. While Taiga usually has more orange on the bill than Tundra, it should be noted that bill colours and patterns can vary greatly among individual birds.

Having dealt with the complicated group first, the black and white group should be plain sailing … or is it? The key with this group is the face pattern and the underparts. We can forget the complicated and confusing tones of oranges and pinks with these birds because they all have dark bills and legs. The most attractive of the group is the strikingly patterned

Taiga Bean Goose (Martin Garner)

Tundra Bean Geese (Killian Mullarney)

Barnacle Geese *(Richard T. Mills)*

Barnacle Goose. Breeding in Greenland and migrating through Iceland, it's not surprising that the main populations are found along the rugged west coast of Ireland. Lisadell, in Sligo, holds some of the biggest flocks, and with the backdrop of the mighty Benbulben, you might even be inspired to write a little poetry as they drop into the grasslands nearby (it's no wonder W.B. Yeats lived there). Before bird migration was fully understood, it was believed that these birds emerged from barnacles each winter, hence their name. Barnacle Geese show a striking white face against a black head, neck and breast, a stubby black bill and white underparts, with neat grey barring on the flanks. The upperparts show a beautiful pattern of pale grey, black and white barring. These features make Barnacle Geese unmistakeable.

Barnacle Goose *(Clive Timmons)*

Cackling Canada Goose *(Martin Garner)*

Canada Geese are equally distinctive, showing a black head, neck and breast, but with striking white cheeks that extend down to form a white 'chinstrap'. The underparts show a brownish wash, while the upperparts are greyish-brown with indistinct barring. The problem with Canada Geese is that there are many different forms, each varying in size from as small as a Barnacle to as large as a Greylag Goose. The colour can also appear very different, with some being very pale on the breast and others being very dark. Some have complete white chinstraps; others have incomplete ones where the white band does not meet under the chin. In North America, Canada Goose has now been divided into a large-bodied, interior- and southern-breeding species, and a small-bodied tundra-breeding species. The large-bodied group is still known as Canada Goose, while the small-bodied group is now known as Cackling Goose. Add to this the amount of cross-breeding that occurs in wildfowl collections and among feral birds, and it soon emerges that birds can appear in all shapes and sizes. The only true wild Canada Geese that occur in Ireland are birds that arrive with wintering Barnacle or Greenland White-fronted Geese, where their breeding ranges may overlap. You can also tell feral birds because they tend to be less wary than their wilder cousins, which are hunted in North America.

The last in this group, the Brent Goose, will be most familiar to those who live along coastal estuaries. They too have black heads, necks and breasts, but show white neck patches. The upperparts are dark grey, appearing almost black at a distance. The birds that occur in Ireland are referred to as 'pale-bellied' Brent and come from Arctic Canada. As their name suggests, pale-bellied Brent have pale, greyish-brown lower breasts and bellies that contrast with the black breast. The Siberian race is known as 'dark-bellied' Brent and, you've guessed it, has dark lower

An adult Brent Goose *(Clive Timmons)*

breasts and bellies that show little or no contrast with the black breast. Dark-bellied Brent occur in small numbers each year in Ireland, which isn't too surprising given the fact that the birds that occur each winter in Britain are of this race. One last member of the Brent Goose tribe is a North American race known as 'Black Brant'. These have jet-black bellies that show no contrast at all with the black breast. The black of the belly extends down to between the legs and contrasts with a striking white flank stripe. Their upperparts are also black, with no greyish tones. Just like Canada Geese, some taxonomists are reviewing the Brent family and it may well be that three distinct species will be recognised in the future.

Finally, the Snow Goose. This is a North American species and occurs in two distinct colour phases: the 'white' and 'blue' (a colour phase is the equivalent of humans having blue or brown eyes). Both phases show a thick pink bill and pink legs. The white phase (from which the species derives its name) is very easy to identify. They are all white except for black on the wingtips, a feature most easily seen in flight (they have almost the same wing pattern as Gannets). By contrast, the blue phase might well fit into the grey goose category. They show a white head and upper neck, a brownish-grey lower neck, underparts and upperparts, a white ventral area, and contrasting bluish-grey wings. Interestingly, it appears that birds choose mates that are of the same colour phase as their parents, regardless of their own colouration. So a blue phase bird that has white phase parents will only choose a white phase bird for a mate and vice versa. Birds from mixed colour phase parentage will choose either white or blue phase mates.

Caution must always be exercised when identifying a blue phase Snow Goose, as some Greenland White-fronted Geese can hybridise with

A juvenile Brent Goose — note the pale fringes to the feathers on the wings which distinguish it from an adult *(Clive Timmons)*

White phase Snow Geese *(Richard T. Mills)*

white phase Snow Geese and their offspring can look remarkably like 'true-blues'. Widely kept in captivity, the only truly wild Snow Geese that occur in Ireland are usually with Greenland White-fronted Geese, where, like Canada Geese, their breeding ranges may overlap.

Hybrid geese can cause all sorts of identification trouble, but there is yet one more issue to be considered when you think you have found a rare goose. Like ducks, geese are kept in collections and zoos and as a result many can escape. It seems that a lot of exotic geese found in Ireland are deemed, like ducks, 'guilty until proven innocent'. One such example occurred in Wexford in the winter of 1997, when a very rare Siberian bird called a Red-breasted

Goose arrived with a party of Greenland White-fronted Geese. The White-fronted Geese had migrated through Norway before touching down in Wexford. The Red-breasted Goose appeared wary and fed alongside all the other geese. Subsequently, the 'powers-that-be' decided that this beautiful bird was most likely an escapee from a collection and had linked up with the wild geese. I travelled to Wexford to see it at the time and, for me, seeing such a wonderful bird in Ireland was truly magical. Wild or not, watching that bird flying to roost with thousands of other geese against a dramatic sunset on that cold winter's evening still remains one of the best Christmas presents I have ever received.

PART 2

Chapter 20

Ireland's Birds of Prey

Sparrowhawk *(Joe Curtis)*

I was haunted by an image of a bird for almost 15 years. I would open magazines and be visually assaulted by it. Once, when browsing in a bookshop, I discovered it staring out at me from the cover of a new book on rare birds. Worse still, Anthony McGeehan,

Gyr Falcon, North Slob, Co. Wexford *(Anthony McGeehan)*

the photographer who captured this dreaded image, had the cheek to send it to me as a Christmas card, wishing me the very best of the season. That image was of a white phase Gyr Falcon, the ultimate bird of prey. Gyr Falcons have different colour phases, depending on where they originate from; the most beautiful is the Greenland white phase.

Anthony's photograph shows the bird sitting on a fencepost on the North Slob in Wexford, and was a constant reminder that a conspiracy of events had prevented me from ever seeing a Gyr. At the time, I comforted myself with the knowledge that they regularly turn up in Ireland. I was right. Every year since that Wexford bird in April 1986, one or two had been seen … but not by me! That is until November 2000 when a young bird migrating south off Greenland was blown across the Atlantic on the strong north-westerly winds and turned up in Kilcoole, Wicklow. The following morning, I was there. It was worth the wait. I witnessed what could only be described as an avian spectacle as this enormous, powerful falcon performed magnificently. At one stage it flew right over me. The demon was exorcised and Anthony duly forgiven for that Christmas card.

Such 'rapturous' moments are few and far between in Ireland, which suffers from a general lack of raptors (birds of prey). I often wonder what it would be like to live in Spain, where birders are spoilt with four species of vultures; Bonelli's, Booted,

Short-toed and Imperial Eagles; and Black Kites, Honey Buzzards and Lesser Kestrels, to name but a few. We are simply too far north and west to attract birds of prey (or BOPs, as they are also called) from Europe, and many migratory birds will not cross the large expanse of water to reach us.

Until recently, on a very good day in Ireland you might just manage to see five species: Peregrine Falcon, Kestrel, Merlin, Sparrowhawk and Hen Harrier. So bird of prey identification in Ireland should not be too challenging.

Falcons are fast, streamlined hunters with compact bodies and pointed wings, and the family includes the Peregrine, Merlin and Kestrel. The largest is the Peregrine (or 'Perrie', to give them their cool name). These are blue-grey above with a dark hood over the head, and show strong dark markings beneath the eyes, known as 'moustachial stripes'. Their underparts are white-based with dark barring. When hunting, they soar to great heights and circle, watching below for suitable prey before swooping down with closed wings to hit their target. In such

dives, they can reach speeds of over 320 kph, making them the fastest bird in the world. This technique takes some time to perfect, and in autumn it's always fascinating to watch young Perries swoop down on migrating wader flocks, only to pull out of their dive before hitting the ground. Some waders seem to have realised that if they stay in deep water, they won't get hit as the raptors seem very reluctant to get too wet.

To say that a Perrie has great eyesight is an understatement. I've seen one leave a sea-cliff in autumn and fly strongly out to sea. Following it through my telescope, I watched in disbelief as it aimed straight for a Leach's Petrel, snatched it from just above the waves, and returned to enjoy its meal back on the cliffs. The fact that I could just about see the petrel using a telescope is a testament to the sharpness of that bird's eyesight.

Kestrels are the commonest and our most familiar falcon. They are easily distinguished while hunting as these are the birds that hover in the wind, altering their position with slight tail and body movements before dropping down to snatch a small bird, mouse or even

Peregrine *(John Finn)*

Kestrel *(Warren Hewitt)*

an insect. Recent research has shown that Kestrels may be able to see in ultraviolet. What advantage might that have for a bird? Well, rodents are constantly leaving small droplets of urine as scent marks as they work their way along their territory. Such scent marks glow when seen in ultraviolet, allowing Kestrels to follow the route of the unsuspecting rodents below. When perched, the upperparts of the Kestrel appear quite rufous, with the male showing a greyish head and a lovely grey, black-tipped tail. Females are more barred above and show heavy streaking below.

Our smallest falcon is the Merlin, a scarce breeding bird of upland bogs. Males are grey above, while females appear quite brown. Both show heavy streaking below, but neither shows strong moustachial stripes, which makes them easy to separate from Peregrines at a distance. Merlins specialise in the fast chase, hunting low over the ground to flush birds before using their speed and agility to catch their prey. These small falcons seem to have no fear. I've watched a male attack a large female Peregrine that strayed a little too close to its breeding area. Despite the very obvious size difference, this enraged little falcon continuously dive-bombed the larger bird until it left the area.

Sparrowhawks, like Kestrels, are a common sight both in town and countryside. Their rounded wings (a feature of the hawk family) are ideal for flying fast through woodland and over hedgerows. They specialise in the 'surprise attack' strategy and are known to raid the odd bird table and garden feeding station, picking off Greenfinches and Starlings. They are also very daring and will often follow prey headfirst into the densest bushes. And they don't just go after small birds. Sparrowhawks will not hesitate to tackle birds like Woodpigeons, which are bigger and heavier than themselves. Males are the more colourful, with grey upperparts and rich chestnut barring on the underparts. Females are brown above with dark barring on their underparts. Both male and female have yellow-orange eyes.

Perhaps most graceful of all is the Hen Harrier. These are long-winged, long-tailed birds that glide

Merlin *(Breffni Martin)*

Sparrowhawk *(Joe Curtis)*

163

(quarter) on raised wings over marshland, farmland and bogs. Males are pearl-grey above with black wingtips and are white below. Females are brown above with dense streaking below, but show a distinctive white rump, giving them their nickname of 'ringtails'. Males also have a white rump, but this can sometimes be difficult to see against their pale grey upperparts and tail.

In all five species, the females are always considerably larger than the males. This is a defence mechanism against attacks by males on chicks during the breeding season.

In addition to the 'famous five' above, we also have two more Irish breeding raptors. Buzzards have been present for many years in northern counties, having established themselves by crossing over from Scotland into Antrim. Until recently, these large, round-winged, short-tailed birds rarely ventured very far south. However, in the early 1990s, a ban on the use of strychnine for 'vermin' control came into force in the Republic of Ireland. Within a very short space of time, Buzzards began appearing in Donegal and Louth. Now we have Buzzards holding territory and breeding successfully as far south as Wexford and Cork, as well as in many inland counties.

The other Irish breeding raptor is the larger cousin of the Sparrowhawk, the Goshawk. These are perhaps one of the rarest breeding raptors we have and are extremely wary and elusive. In over 30 years of birding, I've only seen Goshawk on a handful of occasions … and it isn't for the want of looking. They are birds of woodland and the best time for seeing them is in early spring when they tend to do aerial displays over their territory (as most BOPs do).

So, is that it? Well, not really, because if you look at the checklist of Irish birds, you'll see that up to 22 raptor species have been recorded. True, some of them, like Spotted Eagle, Lesser Kestrel and Griffon Vulture, were last recorded or collected (the polite word for shot) in the 19th century. However, our proximity to Scotland (the Mull of Kintyre can be seen clearly from Rathlin Island in Antrim) does allow Golden Eagles to make their way over to the coastline of Northern Ireland almost annually. These are usually young birds that have been forced from their parents' territories and are on the move before establishing

Hen Harrier *(Killian Mullarney)*

Buzzard *(John Finn)*

their own. As Golden Eagle numbers increase in Scotland, the incidence of such sightings are likely to increase. Unfortunately, the birds that have been seen tend to be one-day wonders, with only a few staying in an area long enough to be seen by raptor-hungry birders.

Golden Eagles were once a widespread breeding species, with birds still present in Donegal and Mayo in the early 1900s. One pair even bred successfully on Fair Head, Co. Antrim, during the 1950s and up until 1960. Since then, none has attempted to breed. That was until 2005, when a pair of young birds laid the first Golden Eagle egg in the wild for 45 years. In 2007, the first Golden Eagle chick fledged successfully. These birds are part of a reintroduction programme launched as part of the Millennium Project, which has funded the release of Golden Eagles back into the wild in Donegal. Most of these birds have been sourced as nestlings in Scotland, in co-operation with conservation and government bodies there. This project has been very successful, with a high percentage of birds adapting to their new surroundings. It's also crucial that the local farming

Red Kite *(Terry Flanagan)*

communities and organisations are supporting the project. It now seems likely that we will once again be treated to the spectacle of these incredible birds flying in Irish skies. Even better, on foot of the success of the reintroduction of Golden Eagles back into Ireland, their larger cousins, the White-tailed Eagle, are now flying over the skies of Kerry under a similar re-introduction scheme launched in 2007.

Another reintroduction programme currently underway in Scotland was certainly responsible for an increase in the sightings of one of the most handsome of Europe's raptors, the Red Kite. These birds, originating in Northern Europe, have been released into suitable habitats in Scotland on a phased basis. Each bird carries a unique coloured tag on its wing that identifies it. Many of these birds disperse in winter and several were seen in Ireland. Red Kites have truly superb aerial skills, soaring effortlessly on long, broad wings and using their long, orange-red, forked tail to make minute adjustments in speed and direction. They were once a widespread Irish breeding species, but it is considered unlikely that they survived into the 19th century due to persecution and deliberate eradication programmes by gamekeepers. However, pairs of Red Kites have spent several months in the south-west and the north-east in recent years, and were seen displaying as the breeding season approached. These were all wing-tagged birds from the Scottish reintroduction programme and it was hoped that they might establish a territory and breed in Ireland for the first time in hundreds of years. Alas, the birds moved on, but hope springs eternal because in 2007, 30 birds were re-introduced into Wicklow. Once again, Red Kites are flying wild and free in Ireland.

Speaking of spring … May is the month when we can expect to see two of the rarer summer migrant raptors, Marsh Harriers and Ospreys. As their name suggests, Marsh Harriers are true wetland birds. They are usually seen quartering reedbeds and lake fringes, hunting small ducks and Moorhens. They are bigger than Hen Harriers and have broader wings, giving them an almost Buzzard-like appearance. Males are quite attractive, with striking grey, black and brown wings, a pale head and a grey tail. Females are

Marsh Harriers *(Adrian Dancy)*

generally all dark brown with a buff-yellow crown and creamy patches on the forewings. Each summer, several birds turn up but, invariably, these prove to be females (which in the world of harriers always outnumber males). Males that have been seen are usually young birds and for these reasons, breeding opportunities are few. However, I'm convinced that in some years, at quiet, undisturbed locations, Marsh Harriers do occasionally breed.

Likewise, it can only be a matter of time before Ospreys, the great fish-hunters of the raptor world, breed here. Rumours abound that in recent summers, birds have been present in prime breeding locations. Ospreys are large birds that hover over open water before plunging, feet first, into the water to catch fish. If successful, they manoeuvre the fish in their talons to face head-first for better aerodynamics before flying away to eat it. After each dive, they also give their plumage a good shake immediately after emerging from the water. It took me many years to see my first Osprey in Ireland, but in 2000 I saw three different

birds. One was a juvenile bird that was hunting and diving at the Swords Estuary in Dublin. It was interesting to note the reaction of the other birds of the estuary. They all immediately flew away as soon as the Osprey appeared. Ospreys survive on fish alone and this bird posed no threat whatsoever to the other birds on the estuary. In countries where Ospreys are common, the other birds seemed to have learned this lesson and will continue feeding, totally ignoring Ospreys overhead.

Some May days can indeed be magical. One such day I was treated to the wonderful sight of an Osprey hunting over the mountain lakes of Wicklow in the morning, before seeing a Montagu's Harrier, one of the lightest and most acrobatic birds of prey, in the afternoon in north Dublin. This bird was hunting over fields right alongside the M1 motorway. Interestingly, other birders who had spent a day or two watching the

Hobby *(Warren Hewitt)*

Male Red-footed Falcon *(Warren Hewitt)*

occurred, with some reports involving several birds together in a small hunting flock. Males are sooty-grey, while females show a combination of grey, orange-buff and white colouring. As their name suggests, they have red legs and feet as well as a reddish cere (the bare area at the base of the bill). In most other raptors, these parts are yellow on adults and bluish-grey on immatures. Red-footed Falcons feed on insects that they catch on the wing, but also hunt on the ground for larvae and worms. The other wonderful thing about them is that they are usually very tame and approachable.

If asked what my favourite bird of prey is, I will always instantly opt for another migrant falcon, the Hobby. About Kestrel-sized and showing colouration similar to that of Peregrine Falcons, they are the 'top-guns' of the hunters. Swift-like in silhouette due to their long, swept-back wings, a Hobby is capable of chasing and catching Swifts and Swallows in flight. They also catch insects like dragonflies on the wing, transferring their prey from talon to beak as they fly. The strongly streaked underparts and the blood-red thigh feathering on the adults add a dash of colour to their plumage, while their aerial abilities are breath-taking. Interestingly, their Latin name, *Falco subbuteo,* lends its name to the popular table football game, Subbuteo. Apparently the inventor of the game wanted to patent the name of the game as 'The Hobby', but was not allowed. So, he chose the bird's Latin name instead.

Hobby is yet another good candidate for Irish citizenship, with several pairs seen in suitable habitat in recent years. So is it their speed and agility that make Hobby my favourite raptor? Or is it their bold colouring? Well, in truth it's a combination of all these factors, as well as one more very simple explanation: I've been very lucky in seeing many Hobbies in Ireland … unlike my good friend, Anthony. For many years, Hobbies gave me great comfort when confronted by that blasted Gyr photograph. For, just like me with Gyrs, Anthony was jinxed with Hobby. It was his 'bogey bird'.

I'm happy to report that he has finally seen one in Ireland, so we're even for now … until the next big rare one.

Montagu's also saw a Marsh Harrier, several Buzzards and an Osprey, all flying north following the line of the road. Raptors will follow natural lines and features such as rivers when migrating — were these birds using the motorway in the same fashion?

Montagu's Harriers (or 'Monties', to give them their birders' name) are the epitome of graceful hunters. Appearing very similar to Hen Harriers, they can be very easily overlooked but are more rakish and agile in flight. In recent springs and summers, Ireland has experienced a regular arrival of this species, which breeds in Europe and, most years, in Britain. If the pattern of these sightings established over the last few years is anything to go by, my money is on them to become yet another addition to our list of breeding raptors.

Birders are always watching the weather and should we get a sustained flow of easterly winds from central Europe in spring, we may be treated to the gem of the falcon world — a Red-footed Falcon. In some years, up to five of these Kestrel-sized birds have

Chapter 21

Ireland's Owls

Long-eared Owl (*Breffni Martin*)

There are just so many positive aspects to having an interest in, and a little knowledge of, Ireland's birds. Birding is a reasonably healthy pursuit that can be done either outdoors or from the kitchen window. It

Barn Owl (*John Finn*)

gives an insight into the changing season, is challenging when identifying new species, and is tremendously rewarding and enjoyable. However, birding is not a recommended pastime for anyone with an interest in films or television drama when such productions are based in an Irish setting. Why? Invariably there is a night scene and it's then that the dreaded 'too-wit, too-woooo' calls of a Tawny Owl shatter the illusion. Atmospheric as the calls of Tawny Owls are, being a birder I know that the species does not occur in Ireland. I can also guarantee you that there is not an undiscovered colony of Tawny Owls hidden in the Vale of Avoca, despite the nocturnal calls you may have heard during an episode of 'Ballykissangel'.

There are over 200 species of owl in the world. Some are migratory, but the majority are sedentary (that is, they do not migrate). Tawny Owls fall into this latter category, so while they may occur as close as Wales and Scotland, they have not made it across to Ireland. Further to this, as we have already seen in Chapter 1, Ireland has been isolated as an island for over 8,000 years, so the species has never occurred here, not even in the distant past.

Three species of owl do occur and breed in Ireland: the Barn Owl, the Long-eared Owl and the Short-eared Owl. The Barn Owl (sometimes referred to as the 'white owl' in rural areas) is perhaps the best known of the three, having gained stardom on Irish television screens as the owl of 'The Late Late Show' (in the 'old' days, it was a Long-eared Owl). Barn Owls are more often heard than seen, and their calls consist of a variety of shrieks and hisses (most un-owl-like). Many people actually believe that the calls of the Barn Owl are in fact the origins of the dreaded cries of the banshee. When they are seen, Barn Owls are usually ghostly white visions flying across a country road at night … and this is usually the only glimpse we get of these shy birds. However, some occasionally hunt in daylight and it's only then that you can appreciate the beautiful golden-brown upperparts and crown feathers with delicate and intricate patterns of spots, the large black 'seal pup' eyes, and white underparts with varying amounts of buff spotting. Barn Owls belong to a family known as *Tyto* and are considered to be quite different from 'typical' owls. They are also one of the most widely distributed birds in the world, being found in Europe, Asia, Australia, Africa and North and South America.

The most distinctive feature of the *Tyto* owls is their heart-shaped facial disc, which in Barn Owls is strikingly white. The facial disc is formed by layers of stiff, dense feathers that act like a reflector, amplifying sounds (including high frequencies). As Barn Owls have ears positioned asymmetrically (the left ear is higher than the right), they can, by a simple turn of the head, analyse the sounds that travel along the facial disc. By calculating the minute differences in the directions of the sound, they can then accurately

Barn Owl *(John Finn)*

pinpoint potential prey, even if it is out of view. Add to this the large, light-gathering eyes that can see almost twice as well as we can in darkness, the sharp talons, and the specially adapted flight feathers and downy upperwing feathers that eliminate all sound made by the wings, and the result is a highly evolved and formidable nocturnal hunter.

When hunting, Barn Owls patrol over hedgerows and fields with slow wingbeats, head down and legs trailing. If potential prey is spotted, they hover briefly before swooping down, feet first, to grab the prey (usually a rodent). They sometimes adopt a 'sit-and-wait' tactic, sitting on telegraph poles or fence posts, watching and listening for movements before pouncing. Like all owls, Barn Owls regurgitate the undigested bones, fur and skulls of their prey in the form of a dry food pellet. Such items may damage the birds' delicate digestive tracts if processed in the 'normal' way. By examining these pellets, we can get a clear understanding of what the birds have eaten. The presence of such pellets at suitable nesting sites also gives a clear indication of their presence.

Barn Owls have proven to be remarkably adaptable, and I've seen them in recent years hunting for rodents along the verges and centres of newly constructed roads and motorways. They are not restricted to the countryside. Given suitable nesting locations, Barn Owls are quite at home within the city limits, and in Dublin they are frequently seen hunting along the edges of railway lines and canal paths.

The heart-shaped facial disc of a Barn Owl helps it locate the sounds of its prey *(John Finn)*

Barn Owl *(Joe Curtis)*

A Barn Owl flying silently past a rather nervous Pheasant *(John Finn)*

172

Short-eared Owl *(John Finn)*

Despite this, the species is not as common as it once was. Overuse of rat poisons may be having a negative effect on the life-span of many birds, with some ingesting large quantities of poisons each year. There aren't as many old open barns and outhouses in which to nest as there once were, while many of the old hollow trees where they also nested have been felled, because they were either considered unsafe or were in the way of new housing developments. Some farmers, realising the benefits of having Barn Owls on their property, are actively trying to encourage their return by erecting nest-boxes in large trees and outhouses. It seems to be working, with some Barn Owls taking to them in recent years.

Our other two species, the Long-eared and Short-eared Owl, belong to the typical owl family. These differ from the *Tyto* owls by having a round-shaped facial disc instead of a heart-shaped one. Despite their names, the ears of all owls are hidden and the names of these two birds derive from the tufts of feathers on the crown (known as ear tufts), which look like ears. As their names also suggest, the tufts are longer and more obvious on Long-eared Owls than on Short-eared Owls. Both species are very similar in appearance, having a cryptic pattern of black and brown spots and bars on a buff-brown plumage, making for ideal camouflage. This cryptic plumage pattern is another characteristic shared by most members of the typical owl family. Long-eared Owls have orange eyes as opposed to the black-framed yellow eyes of Short-eared, and usually appear browner in colour and tend to perch more upright.

Short-eared Owl *(John Finn)*

Long-eared Owl *(Breffni Martin)*

Of the two, Long-eared is the more widespread and is found in woodlands, where it nests in old squirrel dreys or old crow nests. During the breeding season, the males proclaim their territory by giving a low, muffled 'oo-oo' call that is quite unlike that of the Tawny Owl (film and TV producers, take note). When the young leave the nest, they disperse to different areas of the woodland and begin to give very loud, squeaking contact calls, often referred to as sounding like the 'creaking of a rusty gate'. This allows the parents to locate the young and feed them.

Like Barn Owls, Long-eared Owls hunt by quartering over fields on silent wings or by adopting the sit-and-wait tactic, taking prey ranging from rodents to small birds and even insects. Like Barn Owls, they too cough up food pellets that can tell us a lot about their diet. These pellets are much harder to find, however, as the birds deposit them in woodlands (finding them on the floor of a deserted old building is a much easier task, as in the case of Barn Owls). Long-eared Owls are truly nocturnal, rarely venturing out before dark.

Short-eared Owls, on the other hand, are much more active during the day. Found on open marshlands, bogs and sand-dune systems, the Short-eared Owl is primarily a winter visitor from Iceland and northern Europe. Arriving into Ireland from September onwards, their numbers build up by late December, especially if weather conditions in Europe are particularly bad. By late spring, most have departed again, but some are seen in summer and the species has occasionally bred in Ireland, nesting on the ground (in heather) on open moorlands. In Europe, the diet of breeding Short-eared Owls consists mainly of voles, and it's considered by some that the absence of large numbers of voles in Ireland may be one factor preventing the species from establishing here on a permanent basis. It is interesting to note that the analysis of the pellets at two Irish Short-eared Owl breeding sites in the 1970s revealed that over 70 per cent of their diet consisted of Bank Voles. As this rodent is now slowly spreading north-eastwards (having been introduced into the south-west in the 1960s), it is possible that as it becomes more common, so too will Short-eared Owls.

So is that it? Well, not quite. Three other owl species have been recorded in Ireland. The Scops Owl is a very rare vagrant from the Mediterranean region, where it spends the summer having migrated north from Africa. Looking like miniature Long-eared

174

Long-eared Owl *(John Finn)*

Little Owl *(John Finn)*

Owls, their highly camouflaged plumage renders them almost invisible when perched in a tree. Highly migratory, most records have occurred in spring when birds overshoot their intended destinations (see Chapter 4, 'Epic Journeys'). They feed mainly on insects, but sadly most Scops Owls are either in an exhausted state, dying or dead when found, as they have usually gone too long without food by the time they reach Ireland. Recent records have also involved two different birds being hit by cars — sad endings for such exotic little birds. One was found alive and well on Cape Clear Island, Cork, in the spring of 1999, however, and it stayed on the island for several days.

Another small owl that has been recorded in Ireland is the Little Owl. Breeding across central Europe to the Middle East, Africa and into Asia, this is a very rare visitor to our shores. Most of our records originate from Britain where, in the late 1870s, birds were released to rid areas of various pests (chiefly mice). Little Owls will also take small birds, insects and worms. They are small, large-headed, squat birds and they can be very active during daylight hours. This, along with their preference for sitting out in the open and their loud 'kooooah' call, makes them difficult to ignore if they are present. Alas, despite the

fact that the species is spreading across Britain, Little Owls are also reluctant to cross large expanses of open water; therefore few reach Ireland.

I started on a film theme, and now I find myself back to the same subject when it comes to the crème-de-la-crème of all owls — the Snowy Owl. Owls have gained great popularity recently due to the success of the Harry Potter films, in which they deliver the post to the students of Hogwart's. Having watched some of these films (purely for the ornithological challenge of identifying all of the owl species featured), I note with great interest that Harry Potter himself keeps company with a Snowy Owl. This is one of the largest owl species in the world, standing over 65 cm tall with a wingspan of over 160 cm. Males are pure white with some black spotting. Females are much larger and are also white, with more extensive black barring. With bright yellow eyes and feathered talons the size of a man's fist, they are one of the most impressive birds in the world.

Found on the tundras of northern Europe, Iceland and Greenland, young Snowy Owls are prone to travel south in winter and the species occurred in Ireland on a regular basis until the mid-1950s. Then, for some unknown reason, they simply stopped coming to

Snowy Owl, Co. Mayo *(Michael Davis)*

Ireland. For many Irish birders, Snowy Owl was high on the 'most-wanted' list of birds to see, but few opportunities presented themselves … until the early 1990s. Then a bird spent a day on Achill, in Mayo. Many people travelled to see it, but it was a 'one-day wonder'. It was never seen again. It seemed that once more the species had given us all the slip. Then a bird was found on Arranmore in Donegal. This was a more obliging bird and for those of us who saw it, this was our first encounter with this incredible species. In fact, it took many people (myself included) several trips to Arranmore before eventually seeing the bird. It's hard to imagine how difficult it can be to find such a large white bird sitting out in the open moorland, isn't it? The problem was that strewn across the Arranmore landscape were thousands of white plastic bags filled

with turf, each standing the same height as, and looking remarkably like, a Snowy Owl.

After the Arranmore bird, there followed a series of sightings in the north-west that seemed to involve more than one bird. Then came rumours that birds were actually breeding in the remote valleys of the region. Since then, other rumours have abounded about breeding birds at new locations further south. It now seems certain that we can proudly boast to having Snowy Owl as a truly Irish bird.

Seeing any owl flying across the road or quartering over a field is one of the most magical birding experiences imaginable … and such magic has nothing to do with the 'School of Wizardry'. Harry Potter, eat your heart out!

Chapter 22

Waders, Waders, Everywhere

Redshank and Dunlin *(Annette Cutts)*

Let's face it, birds are not the most fear-inducing group of creatures that live on the Earth, are they? They don't pose any real threat to us; there are no 'man-eaters' among the bird world and none can kill us with a poisonous peck. Yet when it comes to the challenge of identifying some families of bird species, the best word I can use for the feeling that can set in is 'fear'. Perhaps the one group guilty of causing the most fear among birders is waders. Put simply, waders are birds that 'wade' into water or mud, into which they probe with their bills when searching for worms, insects, crustaceans and molluscs. While other birds, like herons and egrets, also wade into water, they would not be classed as 'true waders'. Most waders have long(ish) legs and bills, adaptations to their feeding requirements, but the trouble is that at first glance, they can all look alike.

The problem with the identification of waders lies in the wide variety of plumages that can occur. Adults look totally different in winter than in summer; young birds can look totally different from adults. Then there are those dreaded periods in spring and autumn when moulting adults have traces of both winter and summer plumage. Even worse are the young birds when they begin to moult from their 'juvenile' plumage into their first winter plumage. As

OK, they're waders, but which ones? *(Clive Timmons)*

if that wasn't bad enough, waders can also change shape, appearing long-necked when alert or feeding, and short-necked and hunched when resting. The weather adds an additional complication: birds can appear short-legged and 'fluffed-up' in cold conditions, or sleek and long-legged in hot weather.

There are some people I know who choose to look at waders only when they are in their pristine summer plumage. When it comes to the challenge posed by other plumages, they quickly give up and walk away. However, I suspect that you're made of sterner stuff and will face such challenges head-on.

While over 60 species of wader have been recorded in Ireland, only 11 breed here on a regular basis. Most are winter visitors from their breeding grounds further north in Iceland, Scandinavia and the Arctic tundra (the one exception being the Common Sandpiper, which is a summer visitor only). Many more are autumn passage migrants, that is they only pass through Ireland on migration. Others may be lost vagrants from North America or Siberia. As autumn and winter are the best times for wader-watching, we don't usually have the pleasure of seeing waders in full summer plumage. The best we can hope to see are a few birds that have transformed into their 'Arctic tundra' attire in late spring before they move north. Therefore, we have to concentrate on those returning birds in autumn, when they are most difficult to identify. But the great thing is that many waders feed side-by-side, allowing for direct comparisons to be made.

So where do we start when identifying Ireland's most regularly seen waders? The whole family can be broken into three distinct groups: 1. black-and-white birds; 2. the plovers; and 3. the most difficult group, the brownish-grey and white bunch. The key to wader identification, in my opinion, is to check three crucial things:

- the size of the bird
- the length and shape of the bill
- the colour of the legs

In addition to these, check to see if there are any striking markings, particularly on the underparts (such as streaking or a breast band), and if seen in flight, check if there is a wingbar or perhaps a white rump. Finally, many waders are very vocal and frequently call when in flight. Most give very distinctive calls, so it's always worth noting what the call is like.

After that it's plain sailing because with a combination of these features, identifying the common waders we see in Ireland is easy. So let's take each group one by one.

The Black-and-White Group

The Oystercatcher is the only common member of this group in Ireland. It's a large bird with a bold black-

Oystercatcher *(Mícheál Casey)*

The much rarer Avocet *(Adrian Dancy)*

and-white plumage set against a long, straight, orange bill and pinkish legs. Young birds show duller-coloured bills and legs. However, the combination of these features makes this species unmistakable at all ages. Other candidates for this group would be Avocet and Black-winged Stilt. The former is an occasional winter and spring visitor with a black, up-curved bill and bluish legs, while the latter is a very rare spring and summer visitor from the Mediterranean with extremely long red legs and a thin, black, straight bill. Neither can be confused with the Oystercatcher.

The Plover Group

This group can really be broken into the 'true' plovers and their closely related cousins, the Lapwings. They can best be distinguished from other waders by their short, stubby bills. Twelve different species have been seen in Ireland, but only four are common: Ringed, Grey and Golden Plovers, and the (Northern) Lapwing. Ringed Plover is the smallest and shows a distinct dark breast band (or ring). They have an orange and black bill and bright orange legs. On young birds and adults in winter, this breast band may

Ringed Plover *(Clive Timmons)*

Grey Plover *(Clive Timmons)*

Golden Plovers *(Clive Timmons)*

Turnstone *(Joe Curtis)*

179

Lapwings are also known as 'Green Plovers', or 'Peewits', after their distinctive call *(Annette Cutts)*

be 'broken', appearing as dark smudges on the sides of the breast rather than as a complete band. Our next two species, Grey and Golden Plovers, appear very similar in size and shape. Both are larger than Ringed Plovers and both show black bills, dark legs and black underparts in summer, which turn 'whitish' in winter. As their names suggest, however, the colour of the upperparts is the key feature, being distinctly grey in all plumages on Grey Plover and distinctly golden on Golden Plover. If seen in flight, Grey Plovers also show very striking black 'wingpits' or, to use the correct term, axillaries (another good one for your list). Grey Plovers are also purely coastal species,

while Golden Plovers can be found on inland fields and marshes, as well as coastal areas. The last of this group is the Lapwing, which shows a distinctive, wispy crest on the dark crown and a dark breast band both in summer and winter. Looking at its two old names, the 'Green Plover' and the 'Peewit', gives further good identification tips. While from a distance the upperparts appear all dark, when caught in the sunlight they show a beautiful purple and green iridescence, hence 'Green Plover'. The second name comes from the loud, mournful 'peee-wittt' call they make when alarmed or displaying. Lapwings fly in a very bouncy, lazy manner and show striking black-

and-white underwings that appear to flash 'on and off' when seen at a distance.

With such short bills, plovers tend to pick food from the surface rather than probe into mud for it. As a result, they feed in a stop-start fashion, running, stopping to look for food, and then picking it from the surface. This gives them a very distinctive 'jizz' when compared to other waders.

While not a plover, I will include the Turnstone within this group as they do appear very Ringed Plover-like by showing a breast band and orange legs.

Their all-dark bill is short and pointed, designed for flipping over stones and seaweed in search of insects and small molluscs. In summer, their dull upperpart feathers are replaced by warm chestnut ones, which give them their proper name of Ruddy Turnstones.

The Brownish-grey and White Group

I have saved the most challenging until last. This group encompasses many species that appear very similar and present the real challenge in wader identification. They can be broken down into three sub-

Curlew *(Adrian Dancy)*

Whimbrel *(Tom Shevlin)*

Bar-tailed Godwits *(Anthony McGeehan)*

Black-tailed Godwit *(Clive Timmons)*

groups: large, medium and small. The secret to identifying these waders is to learn one species from each sub-group very well and use those species for comparison as the starting points (by comparing size, bill shapes etc.) when you encounter an unfamiliar wader.

Large: Among the 'large' group is the Curlew, showing a very long, decurved bill (longer on females and shorter on males), a brown, darkly streaked body and a white belly both in summer and winter. The similar Whimbrel is seen in spring and autumn, and in comparison to Curlew is smaller, with a shorter, less

decurved bill and very striking head stripes. The other two members of this group, the Bar-tailed and Black-tailed Godwits, offer a little more of an identification challenge. Both are smaller than Curlew and in autumn and winter show brownish-grey upperparts and white underparts. They can be told apart because the upperparts on Black-tailed are plain and unmarked, while their long, pink-based bill appears almost straight. Bar-tailed, on the other hand, have streaked upperparts and a slightly upcurved bill. Bar-tailed Godwits also show a very obvious supercilium, which extends well behind the eye, while that on Black-tailed is restricted to an area before the eye. In

Bar-tailed Godwits often feed in shallow water on sandflats *(Clive Timmons)*

Black-tailed Godwits often feed in deep water and plunge their heads under the water when feeding *(Eric Dempsey)*

flight, the two can be told apart instantly. Black-tailed show a striking black-and-white pattern on both the tail and wings, while Bar-tailed have unmarked wings and a 'barred' tail (they look like small, straight-billed Curlews). While their body sizes are very similar, Black-tailed Godwits have much longer legs (especially their tibia, i.e. the part of the leg from the knee to the body). For that reason, Black-tailed Godwits appear much larger (taller) than Bar-tailed Godwits. This is a very useful and easy feature to see when the birds are standing side-by-side. The fact that Black-tailed Godwits have longer legs also allows them to wade into deeper water, and it's not unusual to see them wading belly-deep in water and plunging their heads under the water when probing for food. Such feeding behaviour is usually indicative of Black-tailed Godwit, as Bar-tailed Godwits rarely wade into deep water or plunge their heads under water when feeding. There is one final thing that might help with godwit identification and that is habitat choice. Black-tailed Godwits will usually be found in a much wider variety of habitats, ranging from coastal marshes and brackish lagoons to mudflats, while Bar-tailed Godwits tend to favour true coastal estuaries, mudflats and sandflats. In summer, both show a rufous-orange plumage.

Redshank *(Clive Timmons)*

Greenshank *(Sean Cronin)*

Lesser Yellowlegs *(Sean Cronin)*

Wood Sandpiper *(Michael O'Keeffe)*

Medium: The commonest bird of this group is the Redshank, a brownish, streaked bird with a red-based, straight bill and bright red legs from which it takes its name ('by shank's mare'). Leg colour plays an important part with this group. Greenshanks have greenish legs; Redshanks have red legs; while a first cousin of both from North America called a Lesser Yellowlegs has … you've guessed it … yellow legs. It's also very helpful to use Redshanks for size and bill comparisons. Greenshanks stand taller than Redshanks and have longer, slightly upcurved, greyish bills; Spotted Redshanks are also taller, but show a longer, slightly 'drooped' tip to the bill; while Lesser Yellowlegs are smaller than Redshanks and have finer, more delicate bills. In flight, Redshank shows striking white edges to the wings, lacking in all the other 'medium' waders. They also show a white wedge up the back, a feature shared by Greenshanks and Spotted Redshanks, but not by their North American cousin which has a square white rump.

Two more visitors, Wood and Green Sandpipers, fit into this group. Both are smaller than Redshank, have dark, plain upperwings and striking square white rumps. When seen clearly, the greenish legs of the Green Sandpiper compared to the yellowish legs of the Wood Sandpiper clinch the identification. More often than not, however, the only view you might get of these two species is when they flush from a marsh

Ruff — one of the most variable of all waders *(Annette Cutts)*

and fly overhead. All is not lost, though. Green Sandpipers in flight show very dark underwings compared to the pale underwings of Wood Sandpipers. Common Sandpipers are very like Green Sandpipers but have browner upperparts and a long tail that extends beyond the wings. In flight, they show white wingbars and a dark rump.

Another member of this group, the Ruff, can cause the most headaches. The problem is that they can show bright red legs or pale yellowish legs, all-dark bills or red-based ones, and a plumage that can vary greatly. Further to that, males (Ruffs) are bigger than Redshanks, while females (Reeves) are smaller. However, in all plumages, when compared to Redshanks, they show slim, slightly down-curved bills and dark upperpart feathers with distinctive paler edges, creating a 'scalloped' effect. Young Ruffs have warm buff underparts, which make them very similar to Buff-breasted Sandpipers (a regular autumn visitor to Ireland from their Canadian Arctic breeding grounds). By comparison to Ruff, Buff-breasted Sandpipers are much smaller and have a shorter, finer, all-black bill, mustard-yellow legs and a preference for drier areas (they don't like to get their feet wet, if they can help it).

Last of this group are the Snipe and Woodcock. Snipes are a common bird of bogs and wetlands and are most often flushed rather than seen well. When

Snipe *(Anthony McGeehan)*

disturbed, they call loudly and fly off very high in a zig-zag pattern before landing off in the distance. When seen well, they show a striking head pattern, pale stripes on the back and a long, straight bill. Woodcocks are very unusual in that they are a nocturnal wader found in woodlands. Like Snipe, they too have a long, straight bill and a striking head pattern, but their cryptic plumage patterns make them very hard to see during the day as they rest on the woodland floor. At night, they emerge and fly off to feed in nearby fields or around muddy woodland pools. The best time to see them is in early spring when they perform display flights (called 'roding')

over their territories. Both Snipe and Woodcock are resident breeding birds but numbers increase in winter with the arrival of birds from Europe and Iceland. We also get small numbers of Jack Snipe in winter. They are very similar to Snipe but are smaller with a shorter bill. Unlike Snipe, when flushed, Jack Snipes never call, fly slowly and in a straight line, and usually land very close to you again.

Small: Now comes the most difficult group, the small waders (known as 'smalls' by birders). The key bird to learn well in this group is the Dunlin. These are very numerous in autumn and winter, with small numbers

Dunlin in summer plumage *(Clive Timmons)*

Juvenile Dunlin in autumn *(Clive Timmons)*

Moulting Dunlin *(Adrian Dancy)*

Dunlin in winter plumage *(Annette Cutts)*

breeding in Ireland each year. In summer, they show a distinctive black belly and warm brown upperparts; in winter, they appear grey and white. Young birds are brown above and have white underparts, with heavy streaking and spotting on the breast and belly. Dunlins have black legs and usually have long, decurved bills, although some show shorter, straighter bills (there are several different races of Dunlin, showing subtle differences in bill length).

Passage migrants that appear here in autumn include Curlew Sandpipers and Little Stints. In summer plumage, Curlew Sandpipers are chestnut on the head, upperparts and underparts, while summer Little Stints show a rufous wash to the head, the sides of the neck and the upperparts, and white underparts. In autumn, however, the majority of Curlew Sandpipers and Little Stints seen are juvenile birds. Using Dunlin for comparison, juvenile Curlew Sandpipers are taller with clean, unstreaked white underparts, a pale peach wash on the sides of the breast, and a very long, decurved bill (from which the species gets its name). In flight, Curlew Sandpipers show a very obvious white rump that is lacking on Dunlin. Meanwhile, juvenile Little Stints are considerably smaller than Dunlin. They also have unstreaked underparts, but very thin, straight bills.

Curlew Sandpiper *(Sean Cronin)*

Little Stint *(Adrian Dancy)*

Knot *(Annette Cutts)*

Purple Sandpiper *(Anthony McGeehan)*

Sanderlings resemble clockwork toys as they run before waves in search of food *(Clive Timmons)*

Leg colour is also a vital identification clue when watching 'smalls'. For example, Pectoral Sandpipers (a North American vagrant) are about the same size as Dunlin, show similar plumage markings but have bright yellow legs, while Knot (a common winter visitor) appears larger and greyer than Dunlin and have greenish legs. In North America, Knot are known as 'Red Knot', which gives a clue to how different they appear when in their chestnut summer plumage. Other regular North American visitors include Baird's and White-rumped Sandpipers. Both appear very Dunlin-like, but both show straighter bills and longer wings, giving them a very attenuated appearance. As the name suggests, White-rumped Sandpipers show a white rump in flight. If you can learn the plumages of Dunlin, the world of small waders will open up for you.

Lastly, the habitat choice can also provide a good clue. Take Purple Sandpiper and Sanderling, for example, which are both about the same size as Dunlin. Unlike Dunlin, Purple Sandpipers are rarely found on mudflats, preferring to feed among the seaweed-strewn rocks along the coast, where their yellow legs and yellow-based bills make them very easily recognised. Sanderlings spend their lives chasing the waves along beaches and run like wound-up toys.

I accept that waders are indeed a challenge. There are many species not covered here, but entire books have been written on wader identification. We must walk before we can run, and with waders, the same principle applies. It's better to become familiar with the common and more regularly seen waders before tackling the more difficult and rarer species. Autumn and winter are the best times to face the fearsome challenge these birds present. Befriend them and enjoy them. After all, to know them is to love them.

Chapter 23

Thank Heaven for Little Gulls

Iceland Gull *(Derek Charles)*

Some years ago I was in Ecuador, in South America. It's a wonderful country, with rainforests, high mountains and the Amazon. Over 1,000 different species of birds have been recorded there. From a birder's point of view, it is paradise. In two short weeks, I saw almost 500 species of birds — over 100 more than I'd seen in Ireland in 30 years! I saw colourful and exotic birds from trogons to toucans, macaws to antpittas. However, despite seeing all those wonderful birds, I only saw one single species of gull — an Andean Gull. Can you imagine that?

On an average winter's day in Ireland it's not unusual to see up to 11 or more species of gull in one place. So, while Ecuador may have Sword-billed Hummingbirds and Cock-of-the-Rocks, I simply could not live in a country without gulls. As I've already confessed in the chapter on 'Winter Birdwatching', I'm a gull fanatic. I'm at home in Galway docks or watching over the ever-decreasing sewage outflows off our cleaner coasts. Better still is the atmosphere of Killybegs in Donegal when the fishing fleet is in.

What a dump! Gulls everywhere *(Anthony McGeehan)*

From the outset, let's get the terminology correct. Birders never say 'seagull'. In fact, there are very few true 'sea' gulls. While most live along the coast, very few live truly pelagic lives, with the exception of Kittiwakes and Sabine's Gull.

Gull-watching can be very challenging, but unlike little warblers that flit from one tree to the next, gulls are usually very co-operative. They will stand for hours on a mudflat or in a harbour. They will often roost alongside other species, allowing for direct comparisons to be made. The problem is that it can take up to four or five years for some to become full adults. Not only are birders expected to identify the different species of adult gulls, but we are also faced with the challenges of telling young birds apart, as well as being able to identify them during their different moulting periods.

Half the battle in identifying gull species is to estimate what age they are, so it's helpful to understand the 'ageing process' of gulls. This all seems very complicated at first, but in fact it's relatively straightforward. All gulls take several years to reach adulthood. The large gulls, such as Herring Gull, take at least four years, while birds like Black-headed Gulls take three years to reach adulthood. Each year, gulls go through a feather moult, and with each moult they change their appearance slightly. As each year passes, each successive moult brings them closer to adult plumage. Their bill and leg colour also changes each year. Once they reach adult plumage, there is no way to age them — a 20-year-old gull looks exactly the same as a ten-year-old. Birds are aged according to the stages of moult they are at. The different stages are as follows:

Juvenile: This plumage is reached just before the young bird has left the nest. It has its first full set of feathers, but many of the upperpart and head feathers are dull and are designed for camouflage.

1st-winter: This is the bird's first ever winter plumage. This plumage is reached when a juvenile moults some of its body and head feathers (a partial moult) in late summer.

1st-summer: It's the bird's first birthday … it's now one year old. This plumage is reached when the bird

The sequence of ageing in Mediterranean Gulls is similar to other small gulls. 1st-winter plumage (top photo) is darker, and by its second winter (middle photo), many of the darker back and wing feathers have been replaced by pale grey, or white, 'adult-type' feathers. The bottom photo is an adult in winter plumage. The bill (and legs) also acquire adult colouration by their third year *(All photos: Eric Dempsey)*

moults some of its body and head feathers in spring (after the bird's first winter).

2nd-winter: This is the bird's second winter on the planet … it's now a year-and-a-half old. This plumage is reached by a complete moult of wing, body and head feathers just after the summer (the bird's first summer).

2nd-summer: Guess what … it's the bird's second birthday — it's now two years old. In the smaller gulls, such as Black-headed, birds at this age appear quite adult-like. Many birds even show an adult-like hood. Larger gulls still have a long way to go before looking like an adult. This plumage is reached by a partial moult of head and body feathers in spring (after the bird's second winter).

3rd-winter/adult winter: This plumage is reached by a complete moult after the summer (the bird's second summer). In mid-winter, it will be two-and-a-half years old. This is the bird's third winter on the planet. In large gulls, they still show many immature brown feathers and have the dull bills of immature birds. In smaller gulls, they will now be classed as adult winters because they will look exactly the same as an adult. Sometimes the only giveaway with these small gulls may be the fact that the bird's bill isn't as bright as that of a full adult.

3rd-summer/adult summer: This plumage is reached by a partial moult of some head and body feathers in spring. Large gulls are now looking very like adults, but may have some brown wing feathers and black on their bills. Small gulls, on the other hand, are now adult birds and in full breeding plumage for the very first time.

4th-winter/adult winter: This plumage is achieved by a complete moult after summer. In small gulls, this is their adult winter plumage. They now have the full bill and leg colour of adult birds. In large gulls, this is their first full adult-type plumage, with some being almost identical to adults. Like small gulls, the only giveaway to the bird's age might be the fact that the bill may still show some black towards the tip.

4th-summer/adult summer: This plumage is reached by a partial moult of some head and body feathers in spring. All adult summer gulls are at least four years old and for the large gulls, this is their first full adult summer plumage. For the smaller gulls, this will be at least their second breeding season.

Adult winter: This plumage is achieved by a complete moult after summer. All gulls are in full adult winter plumage.

Of course, during the entire course of this process, birds are often in the middle of moulting (transitional moult), so they are sometimes referred to as being in two plumages, i.e. a bird moulting from its 1st-summer plumage to its 2nd-winter plumage would be a 1st-summer/2nd-winter bird.

Larger gulls take up to four years to reach maturity. The top photo shows a 1st-winter Iceland Gull. Although the Iceland Gull in the lower photo looks almost like an adult bird, there are still some darker feathers on the back, and the bill is still similar to the 1st-winter's. The lower bird is therefore a 3rd-winter Iceland Gull *(Top photo: Derek Charles. Bottom photo: Tom Cuffe)*

Adult Herring Gull *(Sean Cronin)*

So, having grasped the ageing concept, it's time to settle down and look at these gulls. To be honest, being a gull fanatic is trendy in birding circles these days, and for good reason. Species that we have taken for granted for many years are suddenly presenting us with new identification challenges. Take, for example, the humble Herring Gull. As discussed in Chapter 13, 'Splitters and Lumpers', birders in Europe have been aware for many years that there were many 'races' of Herring Gull, ranging from Ireland to the Mediterranean, all the way to Siberia, the Caspian Sea and eastwards across Asia. The species also occurs in North America. Most birders knew that there were slight differences in colour tones, leg colour and general shape among the different races. Some were long-winged with slender bills, others were short-winged with thick bills. Some had yellow legs, some didn't. So what? Well, recent research has shown that in many cases, the differences between what we considered races were very significant. It emerged that in some areas where two 'races' breed side-by-side, they didn't interbreed. The vocalisations of the birds were different, the timings of their moults were different, and the plumages of young birds were distinct and recognisable in the field. Added to that were the results of studies into the DNA of these races — not only did they look different, they were also genetically distinct.

In short, the humble Herring Gull has now been split into many different species, and overnight, three new species were added to the list of Ireland's birds.

These immature Herring Gull-type birds all look very similar, but are in fact four separate species. Top: Yellow-legged Gull *(Anthony McGeehan)*. Middle left: Caspian Gull *(Derek Charles)*. Middle right: American Herring Gull *(Michael O'Clery)*. Bottom left: Herring Gull *(Joe Curtis)*. Bottom right: adult Yellow-legged Gull *(Derek Charles)*

These are the Yellow-legged Gull from the Mediterranean, the Caspian Gull from further east, and the American Herring Gull from North America. In the Middle East and Asia, there are even more new species to see.

Birders are suddenly looking anew at these large gulls in the hope of finding some of these 'new' species in Ireland, and when you start looking, it's satisfying to discover that these birds can be found on a regular basis. The commonest is the Yellow-legged Gull which has upperpart colours midway between Herring and Lesser Black-backed Gull, and has, as the name suggests, yellow legs. In fact, so many Yellow-legged Gulls have been found that they are no longer considered an unusual species to be seen in Ireland in winter. It seems that the harder we look, the more we discover and the more we think we know. The more we know, the more we realise that we still have a lot to learn. The 'Herring Gull complex', as it is known, is not for the faint-hearted and many hardened birders have walked way in exasperation.

The largest of our gulls, Great Black-backed Gull *(Michael Finn)*

I use the word 'large' to describe this group, and this term encompasses widespread and common species, such as Herring, Lesser Black-backed and Great Black-backed Gulls. Adults of this group all have yellow bills with a red spot (the 'gonys spot', which chicks peck at to stimulate adults to regurgitate food). Adults also have black wing tips with small white spots on the outer primary feathers. The upperparts vary from pale grey on Herring Gull to dark, slate-grey on the Lesser Black-backed to jet-black on Greater Black-backed. Lesser Black-backed Gull also stands out by having yellow legs, while the other two common large gulls have pinkish/flesh-coloured legs.

By winter, our dumps, docklands and fishing ports are crammed with gulls, all competing aggressively for food among the fish scraps and refuse bags. Searching through the hordes, classic winter species can be detected, two of which are roughly Herring Gull-sized but are referred to as 'Northern Gulls'. These stand out among the crowd because they have white wings as opposed to the black wing tips of the other large gulls. The biggest is the Glaucous Gull. These really can be monsters, sometimes even bigger than Great Black-backed Gulls, and just as bossy — they even have an aggressive look in their eyes. By comparison, the smaller but similar Iceland Gull has a more gentle expression and is not so pugnacious.

Lesser Black-backed Gull *(Eric Dempsey)*

A 1st-winter Glaucous Gull *(Derek Charles)*

One of the 'white-winged' group of gulls, a 1st-winter Iceland Gull *(Eric Dempsey)*

Adult Kumlien's Gull *(Derek Charles)*

Young Glaucous and Iceland Gulls appear pale coffee-coloured with even paler wing tips. By their second birthday, they acquire an almost overall pale plumage (sometimes pure white) before maturing into grey-backed, white wing-tipped adults.

Just to add to the confusion, Iceland Gulls breed in Greenland and Glaucous Gulls breed in Iceland. By January, both species retreat south from the harsh northern winters and reach Ireland in variable numbers. When I started birding many years ago, Glaucous Gulls were by far the more numerous, with only the occasional Iceland Gull being found. In recent years, that trend has been reversed, with Iceland Gulls sometimes outnumbering Glaucous Gulls by as many as 20-to-1 in some places. Why this has happened is unknown, but it may be that Iceland Gulls have had a series of good breeding seasons, or that they are now moving further away to new wintering grounds.

Seeing so many Iceland Gulls is a great treat for Irish birders and, as usual, when you see plenty of them, something different tends to stand out. Several years ago some young Iceland Gulls were seen that showed darker wingtips. Some adults displayed grey spots among the white wingtips. These birds belong to a distinct race of Iceland Gull known as Kumlien's Gull. Every year, a few more Kumlien's Gulls are found. This bird breeds in the high Arctic regions of Baffin Island and north-eastern Quebec and migrates down the eastern seaboard of Canada to winter mainly in Newfoundland. The fact that they turn up in Ireland gives us an indication of the distances gulls are capable of covering.

If Kumlien's Gull is exciting, some winters will be remembered for records of an even more north-western species, Thayer's Gull. This species winters in western North America, mainly in British Columbia, but also as far south as California. Yet, immature birds have been found with the gulls at Belfast dump and Cobh in Cork. In 1998, a superb adult was found with the gulls at Killybegs in Donegal. This bird afforded birders from all over Europe an opportunity to see this rare and difficult-to-identify species first-hand. Killybegs was effectively put on the birding map.

If there are 'large' gulls, there must be 'small' gulls. Small gulls are among the nicest to study. Most take two to three years to mature into full adults, most acquire some form of hood in summer (replaced by a dark spot or smudge during the winter), and most have reddish legs. The great thing about 'small gulls' is that they are relatively straightforward to identify. The most common is the Black-headed Gull (which is used as the comparison species when looking at 'hooded' gulls). These are a widespread species found in many habitats and are worth getting to know because many species that you might see look superficially alike. I believe that half the battle in gull identification is in knowing what the bird isn't, as much as knowing what it is.

Take, for example, the Mediterranean Gull. They appear very similar to our Black-headed Gull in all plumages, but appear chunkier than their Irish cousins and show much brighter red bills. Adults are beautiful birds with pure white wings as opposed to the black-edged wings of Black-headed Gulls. They were once a very rare species to our shores, but in the early 1980s began to expand their range northwards. Today it's not unusual to see up to 40 birds in one place (with Sandycove in Dublin and Cobh in Cork being the 'Med Gull' centres of Ireland). Each winter, birds arrive from Europe; a colour-ringing scheme has revealed that most come from Belgium and Holland. Even more exciting is the fact that in recent years, Mediterranean Gulls have bred and successfully reared young at gull colonies in counties Wexford and Down, and perhaps at other sites in Galway.

Every winter also sees a small number of Little Gulls appear at traditional sites, such as Galway Bay. Breeding in eastern Europe, these tiny, round-winged gulls are always enjoyed by Irish birders. Adults show white upperwings and strikingly dark underwings, creating a very contrasting image in flight. Should we experience easterly gales in winter, Little Gulls will appear along the east coast. Flocks can number several hundreds and are believed to originate from wintering grounds located over the shallow sandbanks in the southern Irish Sea.

Other, much rarer 'hooded' gulls occasionally appear among the Black-headed Gulls in winter, three of which come from North America. Two are very dark on the back and stand out among the gull flocks. The larger of the two is the Laughing Gull, the mocking and cackling calls of which give them their name. The smaller Franklin's Gull evaded Irish birders for many years. Breeding in the prairies of North America, the first Irish bird was found in Kerry in 1993. Since then, many more have been seen. Does this mean that they too are increasing their range, or is it that there are more people out there looking?

The smaller and daintier Bonaparte's Gull is so like our Black-headed Gull that many must be passed over. Franklin's Gull was named after the polar explorer Sir John Franklin, while Bonaparte's Gull was named after Charles Lucian Jules Laurent Bonaparte. Charles was the younger brother of

Summer-plumaged Black-headed Gull *(Anthony McGeehan)*

A 1st-winter Little Gull *(Derek Charles)*

Kittiwake *(Bill Quinn)*

Sabine's Gull *(Anthony McGeehan)*

Bonaparte's Gull *(Anthony McGeehan)*

Laughing Gull *(Tom Cuffe)*

Napoleon and was a great naturalist who spent five years in America when the Battle of Waterloo cast a dark cloud over his work prospects in Europe!

The last of the 'hooded' gulls is one of the two true 'seagulls', the Sabine's Gull. They migrate south from their Arctic Candian breeding sites each autumn and move into the Atlantic Ocean. If caught in strong winds, they can get blown inshore and can then be seen off our headlands and islands. Both adults and young birds have very distinctive wing patterns, with large white triangles on the upperwings. They are usually seen in the company of the other 'seagull', the Kittiwake. Kittiwakes, which are a common breeding species and named after their loud 'kittiiii-wake' calls,

are larger than Sabine's Gulls, have white heads and are grey above with neat black wingtips (as if the tips have been dipped into ink wells). Young Kittiwakes show a strong 'W' pattern on the upperwings, which distinguishes them from Sabine's Gull.

Another ubiquitous species is the Common Gull. Despite its name, it is not the most common gull species found in Ireland. They are very handsome birds, with neat, olive-yellow bills, greenish legs and dark eyes. In the winter of 1979, a very similar bird, called a Ring-billed Gull, was found in Mayo. This was the first Irish record for this North American species and it proved to be the first of many. As their name suggests, Ring-billed Gulls have a broad black

Common Gull *(Michael O'Clery)*

Ring-billed Gull *(Tom Cuffe)*

Ross's Gull — the crème-de-la-crème of gulls
(*Anthony McGeehan*)

Immature Ivory Gull (*Richard T. Mills*)

band on a thick, yellowish bill, as well as having pale yellow eyes (as opposed to the gentle, dark eyes of Common Gulls). In addition, Ring-billed tend to look a little dishevelled, with back feathers often blowing out of place and never appearing quite as sleek as the Common Gulls, among whose ranks they are generally found. It's worth noting that Common Gulls frequently show a ring on their bill in winter, so it is the colour of the eyes and the smaller, neater structure that tells them apart from Ring-billed Gulls. Young birds are very similar, but the larger, thicker bill and the larger size of Ring-billed Gulls help to identify them from Common Gulls.

I've saved the best until last. Like a good wine, the birding community occasionally savours the rare vintage of winter gulls. I'm referring to two species and both are exquisite. They breed in the Arctic Circle and have gained a mythical reputation among birders. The first is the Ivory Gull. Adults are pure white with blue-green bills and black legs. On the other hand, immature birds are not as beautiful, having black spots on a white body and what can only be described as a dirty face. Ivory Gulls are one of the most northern

breeding species in the world and winter on the pack ice. In some winters, birds drift south and make it to Ireland. They are renowned for their tameness (they may never have encountered humans before) and this adds to their appeal.

And then there is the 'gull of all gulls' — the Ross's Gull. Named after the great explorer, Captain James Ross, it was discovered in 1823 by an expedition crossing Arctic Canada in an attempt to find the Northwest Passage. This species ranks as one of the most handsome gulls in the world, showing a delicate, pink-tinged body with a neat black neck-ring in summer. In winter the neck-ring is lost, but the body still shows that distinctive pink colouration. Pale grey wings and a long, wedge-shaped tail are further distinctive features. I firmly believe that Ross's Gulls know how special they are. They always seem to perform to an audience that usually watches in silence, appreciating the graceful moments of a true gem … every bit as beautiful as any bird the Ecuadorian rainforest can offer. You know what they say — beauty is in the eye of the beholder.

Chapter 24

Ireland's Breeding Warblers

Whitethroat *(Sean Cronin)*

Ireland's resident birds have it easy. By late spring, many have started rehearsals so that by May, their songs are perfected and their territories well established. In fact, each morning up to mid-April, they almost have the entire stage to themselves. They are the only show in town!

From mid-April onwards, Irish birds find themselves competing at dawn with a new assortment of singing strangers, the migrants. Some of these strangers have flown over 9,000 km to get here. Many will have crossed the Sahara Desert to reach Ireland. They will also have crossed the open sea, a most dangerous undertaking for any migrant bird. They reach our southern shores and slowly work their way throughout the country.

On arrival, they are eager to establish territories and attract mates. Any male migrant worth his salt knows what he has to do — start singing. In fact, they are so keen to sing, many begin doing so as soon as they make landfall. Headlands and coastal stretches echo with the songs of migrants and for good reason. Our summer migrants do not hold territories on their wintering grounds and don't need to sing until they reach Ireland. It's as though they are bursting to announce their successful arrival. They have waited a long time and have flown a long way to sing. For young birds hatched the previous year, this will be the first time they will ever sing.

Of all the singing migrants, one family stands out as being the most vocal and, at times, one of the most difficult to identify — the warblers. Almost 50 species of warbler have been recorded in Ireland, but this figure includes some vagrant species of North American warblers that have been seen in Ireland, as well as some of the very rare Siberian and Asian species. Most of these rare vagrant birds occur only in autumn, when young birds get lost on migration. In

Chiffchaff *(Anthony McGeehan)*

spring, things are entirely different — birds are returning to Ireland to breed and they are all experienced adults.

Each summer, nine species of warbler can be found in a variety of habitats in Ireland. Warblers are small, insect-eating birds (although they will eat fruit and berries in autumn and winter) and there are several different families that visit us each year. The first group is known as the *Phylloscopus* warblers (birders refer to these as 'Phylloscs'). The literal translation means 'leaf watcher' (derived from ancient Greek) and hence these are known as 'leaf warblers'. As their name suggests, these warblers tend to be found in woodlands and hedgerows and, as a rule, they are usually greenish above and yellowish/white below. Of course, such colour adaptations reflect their preferred habitats. Thankfully, they are also very vocal in spring and early summer.

The three Irish Phylloscs are Chiffchaff, Willow Warbler and Wood Warbler. They are all about Blue Tit-sized, with Wood Warbler being slightly bigger. One of the first migrant singers to arrive in Ireland is the Chiffchaff, named after its repetitive 'chiff-chaff' song. The first Chiffchaffs are usually heard by the end of March, singing from high perches. Willow Warblers usually don't arrive until well into April, and the delicate, descending notes of its song adds a touch of class to the dawn chorus.

Chiffchaffs seem at home in a variety of habitats, from city parks to remote mountainous woodlands, while Willow Warblers prefer hedgerows and copses. When not singing, they can be difficult to tell apart as they are the same size and behave in much the same way. However, look for just one thing — is the tail pumping (wagging)? Chiffchaffs seem to constantly pump or wag their tails; Willow Warblers do this less

Willow Warbler is one of our commonest summer visitors *(Tom Shevlin)*

frequently. Willow Warblers also tend to be more brightly coloured than Chiffchaffs, sporting yellower underparts.

Wood Warblers are the brightest of the three with yellow-green upperparts, long wings and a bright yellow throat and breast that contrasts with the pure white belly. Wood Warblers are rare in Ireland and need large tracts of mature deciduous woodlands in which to breed. Each year, only two or three breeding pairs are found, with the woodlands of Wicklow being a favoured location. Their song is very unusual, with a repeated single note followed by a 'shivering trill'. Male and female Phylloscopus warblers are identical.

The next common group is known as *Sylvia* warblers (coming from the Latin word *silva*, meaning wood). These birds tend to have greyish upperpart colours (the word *sylvia* is like silver, which is greyish … that's how I remember it). Also, unlike all of the other warblers, males and females usually have a different plumage, allowing the sexes to be told from each other.

Perhaps the best known of the *Sylvia* warblers is the Blackcap. These are frequent visitors to the garden in winter, where they feed on apples and berries. However, these birds come from central Europe and will return there in spring. Our breeding birds spend the winter in the Mediterranean countries. The male Blackcap shows the black cap and has greyish upperparts and white underparts. The female has a chestnut-coloured cap and warmer brown upperparts.

Blackcaps like any woodland that has dense undercover from which to sing. Their rich, explosive songs are easily heard, but the singers can be frustratingly difficult to see. They seem to be more common now than they ever were, and it's possible that we have a resident population of birds. The

A Wood Warbler high in the canopy of an Oak tree *(Anthony McGeehan)*

Garden Warbler *(Sean Cronin)*

Blackcap *(John Finn)*

closely related Garden Warbler is much rarer and shyer. It looks like a male Blackcap without the black cap, and male and female are identical. They are as difficult to see on the breeding grounds, preferring to sing from deep cover. Added to that is the problem that the song of both birds is almost identical, and you realise just how difficult Garden Warblers can be to find. To my ears, the song of Garden Warbler is more melodic and quieter than that of Blackcap and lacks the 'scratchy' notes that start every Blackcap song. I'm sure that many are simply passed off as Blackcaps as they also seem to favour the same kind of habitat.

The last of the *Sylvia* warblers is the aptly named Whitethroat. The males are very beautiful birds, with a grey head, warm brown wings and a white throat that contrasts with a pinkish-washed breast. The females tend to show more brownish heads, duller brown wings and a paler breast. These are birds of hedgerows rather than woodlands and thickets, and of all the *Sylvia* warblers, they are the easiest to see. They tend to sing from the highest perches of the bushes and their song sounds like a more intense version of the Dunnock's (of course, you would need to know the song of the Dunnock first).

In reedbeds and wetland fringes, you can find the next group, the *Acrocephalus* warblers (or 'Acros', as birders call them). *Acrocephalus* literally means 'pointed headed' (from Greek) and refers to the shape of the heads of many such warblers, which have long,

sloping foreheads and a pointed rear crown. In general, all Acros are brown above and white below. Some show streaking, others are plain. We have two breeding Acros here and the first, the Sedge Warbler, is one of the commonest migrants of our wetlands. These can be heard from mid-April and, in my opinion, are the jazz musicians of the bird world. Their songs are complicated and diverse, with no two Sedge Warblers ever singing the same song. They encompass a whole range of grating, scratchy sounds intermingled with notes borrowed from other birds.

Sedge Warblers have a very striking white supercilium (stripe over the eye) and will sing from a high or exposed vantage-point. They also show streaking on the back. The other Acro, the Reed Warbler, is slightly larger and appears much plainer, being brown above, white below, with no striking white line above the eye or streaking on the back. They are also the more secretive of the two. They breed only in reedbeds and were once only seen on migration in Ireland. However, over the last 20 years they have colonised the south and east coast counties. Go into any good reedbed in these areas and you'll hear the distinctive, repetitive 'carra-carra' notes of Reed Warblers. In recent years, they have even colonised northern counties as well.

Finally, there is the Grasshopper Warbler, the sole representative of the *Locustella* warblers. It's no coincidence that Grasshopper and '*Locust(ella)*'

Sedge Warbler *(Sean Cronin)*

Reed Warbler *(Richard T. Mills)*

Whitethroat *(Clive Timmons)*

Grasshopper Warbler *(Anthony McGeehan)*

appear in the Latin name of this bird as their song sounds like a cricket or grasshopper. All members of this family have 'insect-like' qualities to their songs. However, many think 'Groppers' (as Grasshopper Warblers are known to birders) sound more like the whirring sound of a fisherman's reel. These are very plain birds with brown, streaked upperparts and whitish underparts that show some streaks and blotches. They are very secretive and can be impossible to see as they sing from deep in cover. They prefer damp areas and will nest in bushes near reeds, lakes and ditches. Of all the warblers we have,

Lesser Whitethroat *(Paul Kelly)*

they are also the ones that will sing during the night — sounds travel best in cold air and perhaps their monotonous song requires both the coolness of the night and the silence of other birds to be heard well.

So, these are the nine species of warbler found in Ireland each summer. Occasionally we do get stray migrants landing in Ireland in spring and, if they are males, they may also be heard in song. This happens when migrants overshoot their intended destinations. In this instance, they are usually southern Mediterranean species, such as Subalpine Warblers. In recent years one species, the Lesser Whitethroat, has actually bred successfully in south Wicklow. These

are *Sylvia* warblers and look very like their cousins, the Whitethroat, but lack the warm tones on the wings and show a very blackish patch on their ear-coverts.

Don't be afraid to tackle this family of birds in spring and summer. There really are only nine of them to remember, and they can be seen in three distinct habitats: woodlands, hedgerows and wetlands. Look for them and tune into them. You'll soon realise that there's really nothing too difficult about them. But most of all, enjoy them this spring and summer. If you don't, you will have to wait a whole year before they return.

Chapter 25

North American Birds in Ireland

American Redstart *(Richard T. Mills)*

In late July or early August, birding in Ireland almost comes to a standstill. The breeding season is at an end and the autumn migration has yet to start. However, all is not as quiet as it seems. The first trickle of waders starts to appear, moving south from breeding grounds in northern Europe, Iceland, Greenland and western Siberia. For those birders prepared to check through such returning flocks, rich rewards can lie in store.

Late summer always produces a small harvest of Nearctic waders (correctly or incorrectly referred to as 'Yankee' waders on these shores). These vagrants are always adults, most still in full summer plumage, and usually associating with Dunlin. The most frequently encountered species at this time of year are Pectoral and White-rumped Sandpipers, with occasional Buff-breasted and Semipalmated Sandpipers, along with American Golden Plover. So are these fresh arrivals from the west? Some people think not, the alternative explanation being that they are birds that arrived in Europe the previous autumn and continued their

Two 'Yankee' waders, Pectoral Sandpiper (left) and Stilt Sandpiper (right), photographed in Derry *(Anthony McGeehan)*

southward migration on the 'wrong side' of the Atlantic. Moving north in spring with European species, they would then have travelled north to the European Arctic where, unless fate dealt them a unique hand, they would have failed to find a mate. As a result, they return south early and arrive with the other 'failed breeders' along our shores. Actually, I think that some late July/early August Yankee waders in Ireland are almost certainly from North America. Those found at the same time in eastern Britain and the continent are probably travelling down from northern Europe.

These early arrivals give Irish birders a chance to sharpen their skills for the autumn ahead. The peak period for seeing Yankee waders is from early September into mid-October. In fact, species such as Pectoral and Buff-breasted Sandpipers occur with such regularity during this period they are no longer even considered to be rarities. Other regular vagrants include White-rumped, Baird's and Semipalmated Sandpipers, along with Lesser Yellowlegs, Long-billed Dowitcher and American Golden Plover. All of these species are the regulars, with anything else constituting a genuine rarity. As a result, species such as Killdeer, Spotted, Stilt, Least and Upland Sandpipers, along with Greater Yellowlegs, will attract a large and appreciative audience. One species, the Wilson's Phalarope, was seen regularly in the 1980s and early 1990s, but for some reason now occurs less frequently. One possible explanation put forward is that the breeding population along the eastern seaboard of North America has decreased.

So far, the least recorded species in Europe are Western Sandpiper and Short-billed Dowitcher. Strangely, one of the most sought-after species is Solitary Sandpiper, which, at the time of writing, has occurred only three times in Ireland, the last being in 1974. Yet this species is seen regularly in Britain. Surely Solitary Sandpipers reach Ireland with the same frequency as our neighbouring island? Perhaps it's easier for Irish birders to look for a wider cross-section of vagrants in 'open' habitats than to rummage through the pools and wet ditches that Solitary Sandpipers like, hence few are found.

One of only three Solitary Sandpipers known to have occurred in Ireland, at Lissagriffin, Co. Cork, in 1971 *(Richard T. Mills)*

The weather systems responsible for transporting waders to this side of the Atlantic are now better understood and have been discussed in detail in Chapter 10, 'Permission to Land?'. The fact that these waders migrate to South America down the Atlantic coast leaves them vulnerable to being blown across the Atlantic by fast-moving, low-level weather systems and even by westerly airflows in the high-altitude jet stream. It is also worth repeating that from September on, the majority of Yankee waders found are young birds making the long migration for the first time.

As also mentioned in Chapter 10, the ability of these birds to have enough stored fat reserves to make such a journey in one flight is just as important a factor as the weather systems that may bring them here. This ability may explain why species such as Greater Yellowlegs, which may be only capable of storing enough fat for a maximum journey of 2,650–2,850 km, is much rarer in Europe than Lesser Yellowlegs, which can store fat reserves to sustain a flight of up to 3,400 km.

There are still a great many things to understand about the occurrence of Yankee waders in Europe. Why, for example, is Long-billed Dowitcher so frequent when Short-billed is so rare? The fat reserves of the latter render them capable of travelling up to 4,300 km, and their migration route has an east-coast bias. Perhaps one explanation lies in the fact that Short-billed is considered an earlier migrant than other species, and therefore may not get caught in the faster-moving depressions typical of late autumn. Another reason is the more northerly breeding range of Long-billed and its great circular route, which loops southward from a higher latitude — again, more likely to experience a lateral wind that carries it out over the Atlantic. Short-billed breeds further south and migrates in hops down the east coast.

No matter how these waders get here each year, they provide some of the best birding in Ireland each autumn. A visiting Swedish birder spent two days with me one September and saw a Long-billed Dowitcher, one Semipalmated, two Pectoral and three Buff-breasted Sandpipers, as well as a Wilson's Phalarope

A Long-billed Dowitcher, Co. Down (Anthony McGeehan)

— more Yankee waders in two days than he had seen in Sweden in ten years! In some years, big falls of waders result in small flocks of Buff-breasted and White-rumped Sandpipers in Ireland. If they ever stay together on the 'wrong side' of the Atlantic, they may even breed some day.

It's not just waders that turn up regularly in Ireland. In some years, we enjoy an arrival of Nearctic passerines ('Yankee flits' or 'Yankee passers', as they are known) and these occurrences make for some of the most exciting birding days ever. Take 25 October 1998, for example. It was a cold, dull and wet day in south-west Ireland. I was birding the Kerry coastline with limited success. Throughout the previous 24 hours, a strong Atlantic storm had lashed the south coast of Ireland with winds of up to 120 kph and torrential rain. It had crossed the Atlantic quickly as a deep depression, so I had high hopes of finding something rare. At 3.15pm my mobile phone rang and a very excited voice at the other end informed me that on Galley Head, Cork, some of the local birders had just found a *Catharus* thrush, most likely a Hermit Thrush, but it was in an exhausted state.

Such calls will cause the average Irish birder a heart attack for the following reasons. First, Hermit Thrush would be a new species to Ireland. Secondly, Galley Head was too far for me to reach before darkness and, thirdly, what about those dreaded

A Hermit Thrush, Cape Clear Island, Cork — a guaranteed heart-stopper for any Irish birder *(Derek Charles)*

words, 'exhausted state'? By nightfall, the identification had been confirmed and the good news was the bird had livened up and was feeding well. Dawn the following morning was wonderful. It was calm, sunny and warm. At 8.05am, the Hermit Thrush emerged and gave stunning views to everyone for three hours before disappearing for good.

Memorable autumn days are often associated with the arrival of fast-moving Atlantic depressions. I saw my first Gray-cheeked Thrush on Cape Clear Island in 1991 when the winds were so strong that — luckily for those stuck on the island — the ferry could not sail. The same was true in reverse with Ireland's only Yellow-bellied Sapsucker (a species of woodpecker) in 1988, with many birders waiting several days for the winds to die down before the ferry would travel from the mainland.

Such encounters can render birders speechless. While I never saw Ireland's first Canada Warbler, which turned up in Clare in the autumn of 2006, I'll always remember the telephone call between the finder of that bird and myself. He was so excited that he was incapable of putting sentences together and eventually handed the phone over to someone else to explain what he had found!

These birds are superstars. They have crossed the Atlantic in dreadful conditions and it's hard not to be impressed by their survival. Unlike other vagrants,

Red-eyed Vireo, photographed on Loop Head, Clare *(Tom Shevlin)*

Yankee passers hold a special place in an Irish birder's heart. The fact that we in Ireland should expect such transatlantic vagrants each year shows the frequency with which they have been occurring in the last two decades. Yet it hasn't always been so. Is it just that there are now more birders, or have the weather systems changed? Undoubtedly, increased observer coverage at prime watch points in the south-west and west has resulted in a greater yield. For example, the first record for Red-eyed Vireo was of a single bird found dead in Wexford in 1951. The next wasn't until 1967, but since then many more have been seen. Other Yankee passers that have occurred on many occasions include Yellow-rumped and Blackpoll Warblers and Rose-breasted Grosbeak. These, along with species like Gray-cheeked Thrush, are the classic, long-distance migrants that wander from the eastern seaboard of Canada. Like waders, they often depart behind a cold front, taking advantage of northerly tailwinds and flying in a southerly direction over the western Atlantic. This is a non-stop flight, and the birds have enough stored fat reserves for a journey that may last in excess of three days.

Problems occur when the birds encounter slower-moving depressions, requiring them to fly through the associated bad weather. Those that make it through continue southwards on their migration, assisted by the gentle easterly tradewinds. However, many birds, especially young birds migrating for the first time, may not negotiate these weather systems successfully and can be drifted out across the Atlantic on the westerly winds. If the systems are fast moving, they can reach the Irish coast in less than 48 hours and make landfall safely. Should the depressions take any longer to cross the Atlantic, those migrants caught up in them probably die in the middle of the churning ocean.

In some years, the weather patterns result in quite spectacular falls of Yankee passers. One such year was 1985, with Cork hosting Europe's first Philadelphia Vireo and Ireland's second American Redstart, feeding within 100 m of each other on Galley Head; two Scarlet Tanagers (second and third records) seen within days of each other in the same small valley at Firkeel; and Ireland's first Indigo Bunting caught and ringed on Cape Clear Island. Other species recorded in that year included single Yellow-rumped and Blackpoll Warblers and a Rose-breasted Grosbeak. October 2005 saw multiple sightings of Chimney Swifts in the south-west, along with Gray-cheeked Thrushes, a Yellow-rumped Warbler and even a Green Heron thrown in for good measure. It's a mouth-watering thought that such weather patterns could conceivably drop hundreds of North American birds on our headlands.

Of course, some birds don't get here under their own steam … some are known to hitch rides. A classic example is a Northern Flicker (another woodpecker) that was seen flying off a liner at Cork Harbour in October 1962. It had landed on the vessel when it was crossing from the United States. The bird stayed on board until it sighted land. It was never seen again. Such 'ship-assisted' migrants are often found close to harbours and ports. This may explain why, for example, a White-throated Sparrow was discovered at Duncrue Street marsh in Belfast in December 1984. People who regularly sail across the Atlantic

Philadelphia Vireo, Co. Cork, 1985 *(Richard T. Mills)*

frequently report sightings of birds landing on ships, so some of the birds seen in Ireland may have been ship-assisted. How can we be really sure that the transatlantic vagrants we do see haven't taken refuge or spent some time resting on board ships? The truth is we don't know for sure, but if they have, you do have to admire their ingenuity.

While the last two decades have produced some quality finds, there are some years when we suffer a Yankee passer drought. In 1998, for example, the Galley Head Hermit Thrush was the only Yankee passer recorded, while none was seen at all in 2002. So, why the apparent fall-off in some years? It certainly isn't coverage — there are now more birders in Ireland than ever before. Furthermore, Europe was still regularly hit with deep Atlantic depressions during these autumns. Was there a problem elsewhere?

The answer could be twofold. First, there may be a population decline in the actual species involved in such migrations. Habitat loss in wintering grounds may be having a drastic effect. Fewer birds migrating obviously results in fewer birds getting lost and reaching our side of the Atlantic. But the mathematics of this theory don't add up: a drop from 11 Yankee passers in 1995 to just one for the autumn of 1998 and none for 2002 doesn't square with the millions of birds that still migrate annually between Canada and South America.

Accordingly, the reasons may instead be caused by shifts in the Atlantic storm track. There is evidence to suggest that the usual fast-moving wave depressions with the associated jet streams that have brought vagrants to Ireland in the recent past can occasionally track in a more northerly direction. As a result, migrants caught in such depressions make landfall in more northern latitudes. This theory may explain the fall-off in some years of Yankee passers in Ireland, coupled with the apparent increase in such vagrants in Iceland. It may be that birders should start concentrating on areas in north-western Ireland in the future, in the hope of finding vagrants. The sad reality is that if such changes in the weather systems become a more consistent feature of autumn, it could make the occurrence of Yankee passers a thing of the past.

Ireland's first Green Heron, seen in Cork in October 2005 *(Tom Shevlin)*

Willet? Some day it will. It can only be a matter of time before one is seen in Ireland *(Eric Dempsey)*

If this turns out to be the case, I rue the lost opportunities of seeing Yellow-rumped Warbler or American Redstart feeding in a garden on an Irish headland. I've missed several Rose-breasted Grosbeaks over the years, but have, until recently, comforted myself with the knowledge that they will occur again. So each Yankee passer I get a chance to see takes on even more significance than it might have ten years earlier. Each one is special as it gives me hope that I might experience the joy of a Yankee passer alive and 'ticking' in Ireland in future years.

I must end by mentioning what species we are still hoping to find. Surely another American wader, the Willet, must occur in some years? The problem is that Ireland has a long Atlantic coastline and very few birders. It's impossible to know just how many North American birds make it to Ireland and remain undiscovered. Who knows, maybe as I write, a Solitary Sandpiper is feeding in some small, muddy pool along the west coast. Muddy pools … hmmm, I know just the place! Watch this space.

EPILOGUE

The World Through the Eyes of a Birder

Willow Warbler *(Sean Cronin)*

I will assume that as you are reading these last few pages of this book, you have some interest in birds and birding. If this book has influenced you to take up birding, then I can only apologise and offer my sympathies. It's time to break some news ... your life will never be the same again. Once you become a birder, you'll always be one. It may take some time to admit to yourself that you are one. It may take even

Siskin — worth being late to work for *(Adrian Dancy)*

longer to 'out' yourself to your friends and family. It may even take some time for you to realise what is happening or has happened to you. But slowly it will dawn on you that you're now seeing the world through the eyes of a birder.

The first hint of this wonderful affliction is when you find yourself watching birds during 'ordinary' moments of the day. You may, for example, start arriving late to work or not getting the kids to school on time. Why? Well, there were Siskins on the nut-feeders ... you love watching Siskins and what's a few minutes in the grand scheme of things? Important telephone conversations are sometimes cut short should you see something unusual in the back garden. At meetings in the office, you find yourself glancing out the window to watch the gulls circling outside and begin identifying them to yourself.

Going for a walk will never be the same again. In fact, for those who walk for the sake of getting aerobically fit, birding isn't for you. While birders walk long distances, it's never in that elbows out, arms swinging, fast-paced manner we all see in our parks and on our streets. No, birders are like plovers — we walk, stop and stare ... walk, stop, listen ... and walk some more. People who walk too fast miss so much, don't you think?

Driving will never be the same again. You'll now drive with one eye on the road and the other on the sky. You'll find yourself craning your neck to look upwards when driving. If you haven't come 'out' as a birder, then your passengers will be really worried about this sudden habit you've developed. In fact, your choice of car will also start depending on how practical it is for birding (never mind the kids or your elderly parents). A sunroof is useful for identifying raptors on wires overhead, for example. The boot must be big enough for a scope and tripod … even better if it's big enough to allow you to keep the legs extended on the tripod to allow for speed of use.

Television and films will never be the same again. As already mentioned in Chapter 21, 'Ireland's Owls', watching a film based in Ireland that uses the calls of a Tawny Owl at night simply ruins the whole film experience. And the problem is not confined to Tawny Owls. Many US-made films use North American birds for their background soundtracks. That's fine if the film is based in North America, but believe me, species like Ground Doves and White-crowned Sparrows were not found singing in Paris during the French Revolution! Likewise, Willow Warblers are not commonly heard in New York. I once watched a film based on a Maeve Binchy novel. It was a nice film, but it seemed that every time the actors walked through Irish woodlands, there were Great Spotted Woodpeckers everywhere. There are no woodpeckers in Ireland! Why is it that film production companies go to such lengths to get the costumes, cars, sets and hairstyles so accurate, but then throw in whatever bird sounds come to hand? It gets even worse when bird sounds are played out of season. One of my favourite books is *A Christmas Carol* by Charles Dickens. In a recent and brilliant film adaptation of this wonderful work, there is a scene where Scrooge is travelling back with the 'Ghost of Christmas Past'. It is Christmas Eve and the young Scrooge is alone in his school. The trees are bare and there is snow all around. It's a perfect Christmas scene, except for one thing … there are Swifts screaming overhead. What are Swifts doing in England on Christmas Eve?

The meaning of news and weather forecasts will never be the same again. For birders, the word 'news' means just one thing: bird news. Yes, the declaration of World War III does have an impact on us, but not as big an impact as hearing of a Bridled Tern a few kilometres away. News becomes your lifeblood. As the weekend approaches, you'll ring the bird

Herring Gull from the office window — Office Tick! *(John Finn)*

White-crowned Sparrow? Not in Paris … *(Eric Dempsey)*

information lines and check out the latest updates on the Internet. This is all vital information as it dictates where you might travel. Of equal importance is the weather forecast. Birders need to see the forecast. We aren't interested in whether it's going to be sunny or wet — we want to know about the wind direction, the arrival of deep Atlantic depressions or cold easterly winds. Sea area forecasts that give the full meteorological situation are what we want to hear. Forecasts and news go hand-in-hand. Understanding and interpreting the forecasts properly will get you to a location where you can create the news.

If you become more consumed by birding, you'll realise that weekends will never be the same again. For most of us, these are precious days set aside for birding. If you become a fanatical birder, you'll find yourself biting your lip when invited to a weekend wedding (especially if it's peak migration time). You'll try everything to get out of it, if you can. If you're forced to go, you will spend the entire day wondering where you might have been and what you might have seen. You'll ring the bird line many times to find out what you've missed. It's torture to hear that a tick is showing itself off to every Tom, Dick and Harry while you are stuck at a stupid wedding. You may smile and put on a brave face, but you vow to yourself that this will be the last wedding you'll attend during any migration period again. From now on, weddings, family gatherings and funerals (except your own) are out from mid-March to the end of May, and from mid-August to the end of October.

Taking holidays will never be the same again. When you book your holiday, you will start checking out the possible species of birds you might see. If on a holiday with family or friends, this may be tolerated by your co-travellers as an interesting aspect to the trip. You'll bring your bins with you (always in the hand luggage — if your main luggage gets lost, at least you have your bins). You may even buy a book on the birds of the area. When you reach your destination, you rush out and explore the local park or the grounds of the hotel while your companions are checking out the local beach, café and bars. You might even find yourself having 'early nights' because you're getting up at dawn to look for birds at the local sewage farm (no holiday is complete without a trip to the local sewage farm). While the others sun themselves on the beach, you start to realise that such

A sunroof is handy for seeing Buzzards *(Mícheál Casey)*

A lovely snowy Christmas scene but despite what film directors will have you believe ... you should never hear Swifts over-head! *(Snow scene: Anthony McGeehan. Swift: Sean Cronin)*

inactivity is truly a waste of good birding time. Getting a tan is less important than getting a tick. In fact, you start to become proud of the white stripe on your otherwise tanned neck caused by wearing your bins. This shows that you've birded in the sun, and this is the mark of a true birder. Anyone who returns from a holiday in the sun with a complete tan (and no white neck stripe) has not done much birding, no matter what they tell you.

Even non-beach holidays can get frustrating. I'm convinced that 'historical sites' bus tours are designed to drive birders insane. Just what was that colourful blue bird that you saw sitting on the wire as the bus sped through that valley? When the bus stops at the historical site, everyone is heading one way while you're walking off in the opposite direction from the main tour. While they are soaking in the history,

you're walking kilometres back the road in the hope of finding that blue bird on the wire. It's always gone when you get there. You return to find that you have delayed the whole tour and that a search party has been raised and out looking for you. Bus tours and birders are lethal combinations — avoid them at all costs.

Slowly but surely, you'll begin to take control over the holiday arrangements and destinations of your family and friends. They will initially be grateful to you for taking on the burden because they don't yet realise you are deciding on the holiday destination based on the possible birds you might see as opposed to the weather, food and beauty of the place. You even decide on dates for your holiday designed to maximise the possibilities for seeing more species. Your friends and family might fall for this once or twice, but when the hotel is dire, the food is bad and the weather is dreadful, you may find you have a revolution on your hands. You aren't worried about these things. You've just spent the entire day at some mosquito-infested marsh and have come away with a load of lifers. What are they complaining about? Your co-travellers (if they are true friends and good family) will be genuinely concerned about you. In your absence, they may even have had a meeting to discuss how best to get you through this illness. For that reason, it's always better to come clean at an early stage of birding. At least your family and friends know what they're dealing with. The truth is: family/friend holidays and birding holidays don't always mix. It takes great negotiations, worthy of the UN Security Council, to secure agreements by all parties before a deposit on a holiday is even placed. Compromise on all sides is required to ensure a peaceful couple of weeks.

One of the great Wonders of the World. No, not the Taj Mahal ... the River Lapwings nearby (*Imagefile*)

You never forget your first Waxwing *(Eric Dempsey)*

there because the nearby Yamuna River is a great place to see River Lapwing, while Indian Skimmer can be found on the Chumbal River (only a stone's throw from the Taj). If you've seen these birds elsewhere on your trip to India, why would you need to set foot near the Taj Mahal? 'Civilian' holiday-makers always amaze birders when they visit countries and waste the opportunity to see so many wonderful birds. Birding really does add an extra dimension to travel.

Even taking plane journeys will never be the same again. While others are pulling down the blinds on the windows to watch a film (which they can hire from their local video store for a few euro), you find yourself staring out the window at the many wonderful habitats that are unfolding below. It's hard not to imagine how many new birds are down there, just waiting to be seen. I can never understand how people don't look down and take in the wonderful landscape below them. Have they lost (or did they ever have) a fascination for what is around and below them?

Finally, friendships will never be the same again. Yes, we all have very close non-birding friends, but birding friends are very special people. These are the people who share (and with whom you want to share) those heart-pounding moments when you see your first Waxwing. These are the people who understand the highs and, more importantly, the lows of birding. They've been there … they really do understand you.

As I said at the very beginning of this book, birding is a truly wonderful and unpredictable pastime. Whether you're a garden birder, a weekend birder or a dedicated twitcher, there is nothing like the moment when you see something new or unexpected. As a birder, the world is full of such moments. It really is even better if such moments are shared with others. There is so much to see and so many places to visit. You'll never be bored again. I consider myself very lucky to be a birder. For me, seeing the world through the eyes of a birder is indeed a privilege. As the old saying goes … 'the world is your Oystercatcher'.

Good birding always.

If you find that compromise is difficult to achieve, then it's time to take the plunge and go on a real birding holiday. Whether you're birding by yourself, with birding friends or on an organised birding holiday with others, you suddenly realise that there's no pressure to make it back in time for the tour bus departure, nor is there a need to worry about whether your family or friends think you've gone missing. You're birding … and it's great! Once you have taken your first real, uncompromised birding holiday, it's hard to go back to any other type. This is what you want to do. To hell with the historical sites … birds are what it's all about. Unless, of course, the historical site in question offers some good birding. Take the Taj Mahal in India, for example. Birders who visit this wonder of the world have no interest whatsoever in the building or its history. No, they go

Appendix 1

75 Essential Birding Terms

The following is a list of birding terms worth learning. It is not an exhaustive list. Knowing the meaning of these terms may help you understand what you are, what others are and what you do. They may also help you understand what the birds are and what they are doing. Part 1 deals with birders and birding, giving terms that are an essential part of speaking 'birder' fluently. Part 2 deals with the birds, their behaviour, their origins and their migration.

Part 1: Birders and Birding

Birder	What you are.
Birdwatcher	What you started off as, and what people think you are.
Birding	What you do.
Birdwatching	What you started doing, and what people think you do.
Bird Fancier	What, under the pain of torture, you must never accept being called.
Bins	Binoculars.
Scope	Telescope.
Pod	Tripod.
Scoping	Looking at birds through your scope.
Digi-scoping	Taking digital images with a camera through your scope.
Record Shot	A poor photograph of a rare bird that at least proves its existence.
Twitching	Going to see a rare bird.
Twitcher	Someone who travels to see rare birds.
Dipping	Not seeing that rare bird.
Ticking	Seeing that rare bird.
List	A list of birds seen — this can be many things, such as an Irish List, a Garden List, a Year List, a Life List etc.

Tick	A species new for any of your lists.
Lifer	A species you've never seen before anywhere in the world.
Year Tick	A species new for your Year List.
Catch-up	A species that is a tick for you but one that has been seen already by your birding rivals.
Armchair Tick	When races of birds are split by taxonomists into different species and you automatically get a tick without moving off your backside.
Taxonomist	A scientist who specialises in the classification of living organisms.
Splitter	A taxonomist who has decreed that a race or races of birds should be split into different species. Splitters give you Armchair Ticks.
Lumper	A taxonomist who has decreed that a species (or a number of species) should no longer be assigned full species status, but should instead be considered just races of one species. Lumpers are the opposite of Splitters … they take ticks away from you. Birders hate Lumpers.
Mega	A really wonderfully rare species to find or see.
Gripping Off	The unacceptable behaviour of someone who has seen a mega and rubs salt into the wound of a person who hasn't.
Being Gripped Off	Being on the receiving end of such behaviour.
Bogey Bird	A bird that you constantly dip on, no matter how many times you have tried to see it.
Stringing	Claiming to see a rare bird when you know it wasn't really one.

Stringer	A person who is constantly claiming to see rare birds that are usually never seen by other birders. You never want to be known as a Stringer.
Hoodwink	A bird that you don't see well enough to be able to identify it. You often suspect that it may have been a real rarity and you are left wondering what might have been.
LBJ	When a 'hoodwink' is a 'Little Brown Job'. Stringers love LBJs because they can be turned into many rare birds.
Suppressing	Finding a rare bird and not telling anyone else about it.
Suppressor	A person who suppresses.
Sniping	Going birding when people are either at work or are unaware that you're even out in the field.
Running	Travelling in someone else's car to go birding or twitching.
Sting	Your share of the petrol costs when you are a runner.
Civilians	Non-birders.
Dudes	What civilians become if they disturb the birds you're looking at.
Jizz	How a bird moves, behaves, stands … it's the bird's 'personality'. Possibly derived from a 'general impression of size and shape' (giss).
BOPs	What birders call 'birds of prey'.
Passerines	Perching birds. These are usually small species, like warblers, finches, buntings. Birds like wildfowl, waders, raptors and owls are non-passerines.
Passers	What birders call passerines.
Yankee Passers	What birders call passerines from North America.
Yankee Waders	What birders call waders from North America.

Sibes	What birders call birds from Asia (many of which breed in Siberia). This is most often used in association with passerines, but can also be used to describe waders from the region.
Smalls	A collective pronoun that refers to a flock of small waders, such as Dunlin. Species like Curlew Sandpipers, Little Stints and rarer Yankee waders are usually found within flocks of smalls.

Part 2: Birds

Singing	The way in which male birds proclaim a territory and attract a mate. (Females do occasionally sing.)
Calls	All other vocalisations made by birds. These can be begging calls, contact calls, alarm calls etc.
Courtship Display	A ritual dance usually performed by both male and female during their courtship. A classic example of such a display would be that of Great Crested Grebes.
Flight Display	This is usually performed by the male over his territory. In birds of prey, it is normally a slow, gliding flight, while birds like Meadow Pipits do a parachuting glide when in song.
Nest	Where birds lay eggs, incubate those eggs and feed their young during the breeding season.
Clutch	Eggs in a nest.
Incubation	Sitting on the eggs to keep them warm, allowing the embryos inside to develop.
Hatching	When young birds emerge from an egg.

Synchronous Hatching	When an entire clutch of eggs hatches almost simultaneously. This occurs when incubation of the eggs commences only after the last egg has been laid.
Asynchronous Hatching	When the entire clutch of eggs hatches at different times. This occurs when the eggs are incubated as they are laid, so that the first egg laid will hatch first.
Chick	A young bird. Chicks can be either totally bald or have down feathers.
Brood	A group of young birds in a nest (or out of the nest, in the case of water birds) and all from the same clutch.
Fledgling	A young bird with its first set of feathers.
Roosting	When birds either sleep at night or rest up. In the case of birds like waders, they roost during periods of high tide when feeding is impossible.
Resident	A species that does not migrate.
Migrant	A species that migrates from one location to another in search of food. Most migration takes place in spring and autumn.
Passage Migrant	A species that simply passes through en route to another destination in spring or autumn. A good example is Whimbrel, which neither breeds nor winters in Ireland but passes through Ireland in spring and autumn.
Ship-assisted Migrants	A species that has spent time on board a ship at sea. Some North American species are known to land on ships in mid-Atlantic and fly ashore as soon as the ship reaches its destination.
Overshoot Migration	When birds overshoot their intended destination during the migration season. This can happen in spring when good weather allows birds to fly further north than they usually would.
Vagrant	A bird that would not normally occur as a migrant or a passage migrant. Most vagrants are well off course.
Fall	When large numbers of migrants are grounded by adverse weather conditions in spring and autumn. It appears that they are 'falling' from the sky.
Feral	A domesticated species that is now living wild. Birds such as Greylag and Canada Geese have feral populations, but originate from wildfowl collections.
Bird Species	A type of bird that can reproduce itself and produce fertile young as well as being genetically different from other similar types of bird.
Raptor	A bird of prey.
Cere	The bare part at the base of a bird of prey's bill.
Moult	The natural changing of birds' feathers. All birds moult at least once a year.
Remiges	A bird's wing feathers.
Rectrices	A bird's tail feathers.

Appendix 2

Useful Telephone Numbers and Websites

Telephone Information Lines

Birds of Ireland News Service (BINS)
BINS offers an up-to-the-minute news service on rare and unusual bird sightings around the country.
Republic of Ireland: 1550 111 700
Weekly Summary of News: 1550 111 701
Calls to these information lines are charged at premium rates.
To report news to BINS: 00353/01 8307 364

Flightline
Flightline offers a nightly round-up of local news for Northern Ireland. Contact: 0044/048 9146 7408

Irish Birdwatching Websites

www.birdsireland.com
The Birds of Ireland News Service website. Provides information on hiring a bird guide, planning a trip, rare bird sightings and photographic galleries.

www.birdwatchireland.ie
Ireland's leading bird conservation organisation. Join online, conservation projects, online shop. Access to all local branch websites.

www.countynaturetrust.tripod.com
Irish wildlife conservation.

www.rspb.org.uk
Bird conservation in Northern Ireland.

www.wwt.org.uk
Wildfowl and Wetlands Trust, with reserves in Northern Ireland.

www.ispca.ie
Local contacts for care of sick or injured birds in Ireland.

www.cr-birding.be
Database of colour-ringing schemes around the world.

www.rte.ie/mooney
Website of 'The Mooney Show' on RTÉ Radio 1, which has many useful bird-related resources.

Bird Photography

www.irishbirdimages.com
Bird photography by Paul Kelly.

www.iol.ie/~birdsgalway/
Bird and wildlife photography by Tom Cuffe.

www.pbase.com/derekcharles
Bird photography by Derek Charles.

www.michaelfinnphotography.com
Bird and wildlife photography by Michael Finn.

www.wildlifesnaps.com
Bird and wildlife photography by Tom Shevlin.

www.valerieosullivan.com
Nature and bird photography by Valerie O'Sullivan

www.flickr.com/photos/sean_cronin/all
Bird photography by Sean Cronin

Weather

www.met.ie
Weather forecasts from Met Éireann, the Irish Meteorological Office.

Appendix 3

Recommended Reading

Birds in Ireland by Clive Hutchinson (T&AD Poyser, 1989).

The Complete Guide to Ireland's Birds (2nd ed.) by Eric Dempsey & Michael O'Clery (Gill & Macmillan, 2002).

The Pocket Guide to the Common Birds of Ireland by Eric Dempsey & Michael O'Clery (Gill & Macmillan, 1995).

Finding Birds in Ireland – The Complete Guide by Eric Dempsey & Michael O'Clery (Gill & Macmillan, 2007).

Collins Bird Guide by Killian Mullarney, Lars Svensson, Dan Zetterström and Peter Grant (HarperCollins, 1999).

Ireland's Lost Birds by Gordon D'Arcy (Four Courts Press, 1999).

Birds and Weather, A Birdwatchers Guide by Stephen Moss (Hamlyn, 1995).

Rare Birds in Britain & Ireland, A Photographic Record by David Cottridge and Keith Vinicombe.

Bill Oddie's Little Black Bird Book by Bill Oddie (Eyre Methuen Ltd, 1980).

A Dictionary of Scientific Bird Names by James A. Jobling (Oxford University Press, 1991).

Irish Bird Report. Published annually in *Irish Birds* by BirdWatch Ireland.

Northern Ireland Bird Report. Published by The Northern Ireland Birdwatchers Association.

The Migration Atlas: Movements of the Birds of Britain and Ireland, BTO. (T&AD Poyser, 2002).

Species Index